FOXTROT IN KANDAHAR

FOXTROT IN KANDAHAR

Savas Beatie

California

A Memoir of a CIA Officer in
Afghanistan at the Inception of
America's Longest War

Duane Evans

Library of Congress Cataloging-in-Publication Data

Names: Evans, Duane, 1956- author.
Title: Foxtrot in Kandahar: A Memoir of a CIA Officer in Afghanistan at the Inception of America's Longest War / by Duane Evans.
Other titles: Memoir of a CIA Officer in Afghanistan at the Inception of America's Longest War
Description: El Dorado Hills, California : Savas Beatie Publishers, [2017] | Identifiers: LCCN 2017021615| ISBN 9781611213577 (alk. paper) | ISBN 9781611213584 (ebk.)
Subjects: LCSH: Evans, Duane, 1956- | Afghan War, 2001---Personal narratives, American. | Intelligence officers--United States--Biography | Afghan War, 2001--Campaigns--Afghanistan--Kandahar. | Afghan War, 2001--Secret service--United States. | Taliban. | War on Terrorism, 2001-2009--Personal narratives, American. | United States. Central Intelligence Agency--Biography. | Special operations (Military science)--Pakistan. | Special operations (Military science)--Afghanistan--Kandahâar.
Classification: LCC DS371.413 .E87 2017 | DDC 958.104/740973--dc23
LC record available at https://lccn.loc.gov/2017021615

First Edition, First Printing

SB

Savas Beatie LLC
989 Governor Drive, Suite 102
El Dorado Hills, CA 95762
Phone: 916-941-6896
(web) www.savasbeatie.com
(E-mail) sales@savasbeatie.com

Our titles are available at special discounts for bulk purchases. For more details, contact us us at sales@savasbeatie.com.

To my parents Jim and Mariah Evans,
In loving memory.

"You are the bows from which your children
as living arrows are sent forth."

— Khalil Gibran, *The Prophet*

Duane Evans in Afghanistan, November 2001.

Table of Contents

Table of Contents (continued)

A gallery of photos follows page 78

Preface

This MEMOIR IS MY attempt to describe the events that I experienced during my service in Afghanistan in the fall of 2001. The feelings of pride in my colleagues, my Agency, and my country that these events engendered motivated me to begin this project and were a sustaining force throughout. My decision to write this story was also no doubt influenced by the fact that my experience in Afghanistan was the high point of my CIA career and the greatest adventure of my life. I appreciated this even as I lived it, and neither the passage of time nor subsequent events have changed my feelings.

As someone whose career often involved a tremendous amount of writing, and having more recently authored a novel, the extraordinary events I experienced firsthand provided material that was hard for anyone considering themself a writer to ignore. Nonetheless, I did just that for several years, even though I had drafted a lengthy summary of the key events soon after returning home. This recollection eventually would serve as the backbone of the memoir.

I understand that a memoir at its best is a great sharing, and at its worst, a great effort in self-promotion. My goal was the first: to share, to the extent possible within the bounds of national security, the personal story that I lived in 2001 beginning with the terrorist attacks on September 11th carrying through to the fall of Kandahar on December 7th. I believe I have accomplished that goal. Still, because I did write about myself I could not help but worry that my story might be judged as self-promotion—something I have witnessed in the professional world all too often. This concern bothered me a great deal, and in fact delayed me from pursuing publication of the memoir. Over time, however, and after reading the memoirs of other writers, I concluded there just is no good way to write a memoir without embedding oneself, the writer, into the story. It wouldn't be a memoir, otherwise.

Ultimately, I overcame my misgivings because I believed that the story was important and shed light on the early days of what is often referred to as "the war on terror." While I still read references to this period as being during "the American invasion of Afghanistan," one of the things that I hope this memoir makes clear is that there never was an American invasion of Afghanistan, in 2001 or after. I even considered titling this book "A Memoir of the Invasion that Wasn't" just to make that point up front. Yes, there was American military involvement in Afghanistan in 2001, but a handful of small, combined CIA-Special Forces teams scattered across Afghanistan working with resistance fighters, even when supported by U.S. air power, does not an invasion make. In fact, the most significant and usually overlooked aspect of the overthrow of the Taliban government and the smashing of al-Qa'ida fighters in the country in 2001 was that it was not achieved, or ever intended to be achieved, by U.S. forces storming enemy strongholds. Instead, it was achieved by Afghan-Muslims, who with U.S. support carried the day on the ground in the fight against terror and tyranny.

For privacy and personal security reasons, when I refer to others in the book who were with me or otherwise part of my story I usually refer to them by their true first name only, though in a couple of cases I use alias names to designate individuals. Also, in a few instances I refer to persons by their positions only. Finally, there are a couple of other instances where I use the true first and last names. In those cases, the persons in question are already public figures due to positions they have held or books they have authored. For these reasons, I trust readers will understand why the publisher and I agreed to omit an index for this work.

Regarding dialogue, while I strove to reflect the conversations as accurately as possible, because I had no means or reason to record these conversations when they happened, all dialogue, even when enclosed in quotation marks, should be taken only as approximations of the conversations or statements represented. The quotation marks are used for writing convention only.

As noted in the statement in the front of this book, which is required to be included in any publication written by a current or former CIA officer, the contents of this memoir were reviewed by the CIA's Publication Review Board (PRB) to insure no classified information is contained herein. My experience in getting this publication approved was generally not difficult, with only a few points of contention regarding the content I proposed to include. I believe the relatively problem-free process was due to the fair review the material was given, and because I tried to ensure there was no information in the manuscript the PRB would likely disallow on a security basis.

The story that follows is my story as I experienced it. It is largely based on my memory of the events I lived through. My goal was to keep my writing as close as possible to what I personally saw, felt, said, heard, thought, or believed. To my mind these are the key elements of a true memoir. This is not an academic study and should not be considered as such. However, before retiring, I did have the opportunity to read the CIA's official, classified history of the Agency teams operating in Afghanistan in 2001, and therefore I was able to ensure that my telling of the story of Foxtrot team—the team that I led from start to finish—is historically accurate.

During the time frame covered in the book, in addition to Foxtrot team, there were six other CIA teams in Afghanistan, five of which were located in the northern half of the country. My focus was on Foxtrot team, although I do include some information about Echo team, with which I was briefly associated and which like Foxtrot operated in the south. The other teams, to which I make only fleeting reference in the book, all performed valiant service for their country and were made up of great Americans, but their stories are their own to tell, should they choose to do so.

Glossary of Acronyms

CCE: Command and Control Element (Special Forces)
COS: Chief of Station (CIA)
CT: Counterterrorism
CTC: Counterterrorist Center (CIA)
CTC/SO: Counterterrorist Center/Special Operations
DCOS: Deputy Chief of Station
DEA: Drug Enforcement Agency
DOD: Department of Defense
ISI: Inter-Services Intelligence Directorate (Pakistan)
MEU: Marine Expeditionary Unit
MRE: Meal Ready to Eat
NALT: Northern Alliance Liaison Team
NE Div.: Near East and South Asia Division (CIA)
ODA: Operational Detachment Alpha (Special Forces "A" Team)
OTS: Office of Technical Services (CIA)
PM: Paramilitary
RPG: Rocket Propelled Grenade
SAD: Special Activities Division (CIA)
SF: Special Forces (Green Berets)
SO: Special Operations
SOFLAM: Special Operations Forces Laser Marker
TDY: Temporary Duty

Prologue

My RUCKSACK WAS HUGE and heavily packed, and I strained to lift it onto the bed of the waiting truck. The other members of CIA's Echo team were equally laden, their packs bulging to their limits. Each of us carried clothing, weapons, and equipment, including armored vests, extra ammunition, communications gear, and medical supplies. The U.S. Army Special Forces team embedded with us was similarly weighted down. For the moment, we were beasts of burden if nothing else.

In an hour the truck would transport us to an Air Force MC-130 that sat waiting at a nearby Pakistani airfield. Its job was to carry us to a remote rendezvous point where we would land and cross-load to helicopters for the final leg of a nighttime flight over the border and deep into southern Afghanistan. It was the big event, and we were more than ready to go.

As we continued to load our gear, Greg, the Echo team leader, returned from the final planning meeting with the Air Force's 20th Special Operations Squadron and pulled me aside.

"Bad news. We have too much gear, too many people, and not enough birds. Between the SF team and Echo team the loadmaster says we have to leave some gear behind plus three passengers."

I braced for what I suspected was coming.

"I talked with Jason. He's pulling two of his SF'ers. You'll be Echo team's stay behind guy."

A gut punch would have been preferable to those words. I was crushed, devastated to my core. But I didn't argue. I'd been here before, ready to go but not going. Greg's decision made sense. The rest of Echo team, with the exception of our physician assistant, was made up of CIA paramilitary officers with current, well-honed military skills. I was a CIA case officer, and my once respectable martial skills had atrophied long ago.

Reading how I was feeling, Greg tried to soften the blow: "Don't sweat it. We'll get you and the other two in on a resupply flight in a few days."

"Alright. We'll be standing by," I told him.

I walked back to the truck and asked one of my teammates to hand me back my rucksack. I carried it inside our barracks then returned to help with the rest of the loading. Now more of an observer than a participant, I paused to take in the scene.

Underneath a canopy of bright blue sky, my teammates were lined up behind the truck waiting their turn to hand up their gear. Clothed in cargo pants, REI shirts, baseball caps, and hiking boots, they might have easily been mistaken for members of a trekking expedition—except for the Glock pistols they wore on their belts and the AK-47 rifles that hung off their shoulders. With only hours left before going into the heartland of the Taliban, gone was the usual light-hearted banter, and each man wore a serious expression on his bearded face. Despite the danger they knew awaited them, they continued working, moving closer and closer with each rucksack passed to whatever fate had in store. Nothing was going to stop them, not even fear.

A surge of pride suddenly swept through me as I stood watching. Like a rogue wave on a calm ocean, intense and overpowering, it took me by surprise and brought unexpected tears to my eyes. In that moment, I understood how such a feeling must have stirred Francis Scott Key to pen the words of the Star Spangled Banner as he watched the bombardment of the stalwart Ft. McHenry by attacking British forces. Feelings that intense needed an outlet.

Although no lyrics suitable for an anthem sprung to my mind, I did wish that I could somehow convey the scene and my sentiments to the Agency employees back home and say to them, "Hey, look! These are our guys! They're the CIA! Look at what they're doing. For CIA and for our country, this small band of men is going after al-Qa'ida deep in the badlands of Afghanistan."

I felt the same about the Special Forces team. Everyone there was a great American, a true patriot by any measure, and it made no difference if he were military or CIA.

Not wanting to embarrass myself with the unexpected emotion, I decided it was a good time to go find Hamid Karzai, or "Mr. K," as he was often referred to among the team, and say my reluctant goodbyes. Karzai, a respected Pashtun tribal leader, was considered key to our long-term success in Afghanistan. As I walked back to his room, it dawned on me that he didn't have an armored vest, and the only thing between him and a steel-jacketed bullet would be his cotton tunic. It wasn't hard to imagine how that contest would turn out. I stopped by my room and grabbed mine.

I found Karzai sitting on his cot packing, his belongings haphazardly scattered about him. I explained that I wouldn't be going with him, but hopefully would join him and the other Echo team members later. I held up the weighty vest.

"Promise me you will wear this."

"Oh, yes, thank you. I will wear it, most assuredly," he responded in his classic Karzai polite-speak.

I smiled and gave him an embrace. "Take care of yourself," I said, and I really meant it.

After saying our goodbyes, I headed down the deserted hall pondering my new situation. Stepping into the light of the afternoon sun, I couldn't shake the feeling that despite all my efforts to get to this point, I might never set foot in Afghanistan or see Karzai again.

PART ONE

HEADQUARTERS

Afghanistan

Kyrgyzstan

Tashkent

Uzbekistan

China

Tajikistan

Turkmenistan

Mazar-i-Sharif

Kunduz

Meymaneh

Bamian

Bagram

Asadabad

Herat

Khadir

Kabul

Jalalabad

Afghanistan

Islamabad

Anar Dara

Farah

Tarin Kowt

Kandahar

Zaranj

Quetta

Iran

Pakistan

India

Capital ◎

City ○

0   Kilometers   500

0   Miles   500

N

1

Outrage

At A SIDEWALK TABLE in Washington, DC, across the street from FBI Headquarters, I sipped a cappuccino and soaked in the perfect September weather. It had been only a month since I had completed a tour as a CIA Chief of Station in South America, and I was still adjusting to life back in the States. Beautiful mornings like this certainly helped. I checked my watch and glanced at the side entrance to the FBI building where I would soon meet with Special Agent Frank Ortiz and the Latin American delegation he was escorting.

I was looking forward to seeing Frank again. He had been an integral part of my station, and we had worked together closely on international terrorism issues. An important part of that work included educating host government officials on the terrorist threat, hence the delegation's visit to receive FBI and CIA briefings in Washington. Frank, who was still serving at the station, had organized the trip.

Although I was still on leave status, I was happy to accept Frank's invitation to join him and the delegation. I was slated to begin working at the FBI in a couple months as a CIA liaison officer, so this would give me a sneak preview of the place. It would also give me a chance to catch up with Frank. In the previous two years, we had become close. Working counterterrorism (CT) operations overseas has a way of doing that to people, no matter which agencies pay their salaries. In the CT business the hours are long with much of the work taking place at night after already putting in a full day. It is the rare weekend that doesn't include working overtime. With the exception of a frustrated spouse here and there, no one complains. Not only is the CT mission vitally important, work against this complex and lethal threat is unparalleled in terms of personal challenge and excitement. In Frank's and my case, not only did the intensity of the CT work bind us together, but other events had forged our close relationship. In one instance, the country where we were serving had experienced an attempted coup. Although the attempt failed, the tension and uncertainty that it generated was nonetheless a memory maker for both of us.

Other dramatic experiences included the emergency medical evacuation of a station colleague who suffered a life-threatening medical event, and the tragic death of Frank's father who collapsed and died during a family visit. I was at the emergency room as the doctors tried unsuccessfully to revive his beloved father as Frank looked on. The strength and steadfast demeanor showed by Frank during that personal ordeal was extraordinary but not surprising given his strong personal character and his intense religious faith. On this cloudless September morning in Washington, I would never have believed that within minutes Frank and I would yet again share an experience neither of us would ever forget.

At about 8:30 a.m. I tossed the empty cappuccino cup in the waste can and crossed the street to the side entrance of FBI Headquarters. Within a few minutes a van pulled up; Frank and the delegation members climbed out.

Frank was the first to emerge, and he gave me a warm embrace. "Hey brother, I'm glad you came."

"Are you kidding? I wouldn't have missed it for the world."

"¿Jefe, como anda?" called out Ernesto Perez, one of the security officials in the delegation. I knew Ernesto well and was glad to see that he was part of the group.

"Bien, Ernesto. ¡Qué bueno verte de nuevo!"

Since my return from South America I had not spoken any Spanish, and the warm greetings that this particularly gregarious bunch began to pour at me in rapid-fire fashion put me through my Spanish-language paces.

We were scheduled to begin the tour at 9:00 a.m., and Frank ushered us into the building around 8:50. At the visitor control point we received guest badges and then took the elevator to the Operations Center, the FBI's focal point for monitoring activities and important developments across the globe.

Oddly, the person who was scheduled to brief us could not be found, and soon it became apparent that something out of the ordinary was going on. The Ops Center was in high gear with people moving about quickly and multiple phones ringing. To our surprise, FBI Director Robert Mueller entered the room and briskly strode past us, a look of consternation on his face.

Before long, an FBI official came and informed Frank and I that a plane had crashed into one of the World Trade Center Towers, and he asked us to escort the foreign delegation out of the Ops Center. There would be no briefing or tour that morning. Receiving no other details about the incident, we assumed it was probably a small private plane that had hit the building. We decided to take the delegation downstairs to the FBI cafeteria until we could sort out what to do about the abrupt change in schedule.

A handful of FBI employees with coffee cups in hand were standing in the cafeteria watching a television mounted on a wall tuned to the unfolding news story in New York. We were shocked to see the images of flames and smoke billowing out of the North Tower. The scenes instantly disproved our previous assumption that it was a small plane and explained the high state of alert upstairs.

Just as we began to understand the enormity of the disaster that was taking place at the North Tower, we saw that the South Tower had just been struck as well, making the fact that the U.S. was under attack plainly clear.

I knew at that instant that al-Qa'ida was behind what was happening. It was exactly the kind of attack for which al-Qa'ida strove—spectacular, simultaneous strikes resulting in mass casualties of innocent people. Watching the screen, it was painfully obvious the terrorist group had succeeded in its goal.

There was little talking among the group of people now gathered in the cafeteria, except for the occasional murmur of "Oh, my God" or some similar expression of shock and disbelief. When the North Tower crumbled there was an audible reaction of horror. Later, when the second tower collapsed, the reaction was more muted. We were too stunned to say anything.

I have just witnessed the death of thousands of people, I thought to myself. It was like a nightmare. I knew, however, that no matter how much I wished otherwise, this was not a dream, and I said a silent prayer for all those souls that had been taken so violently from this life. It was a prayer I would say many times in the days ahead.

Standing in the cafeteria watching the news reports with my stunned friends, I began to comprehend the implications of this outrageous act. I believed it would mean war, and I was certain I knew who the enemy was. Al-Qa'ida had declared itself the enemy of the United States long before this day—September 11, 2001—and had proven it with deadly attacks against the U.S.S. *Cole* and two U.S. embassies in Africa. I had visited one of those embassies only a month before it was bombed. In fact, I had stood in the exact spot where the bomb-laden truck would later detonate. Ironically, I had been standing there having a conversation with an embassy official about my concerns regarding the security vulnerabilities of the facility. His response: "Yeah, we know. The Ambassador has tried to get State Department approvals to move the embassy to a more secure location but with no success. Nothing will be done until this embassy is blown down."

Where the Africa embassy bombings and that of the *Cole* had apparently failed in making clear al-Qa'ida's sincerity in its declaration of war, I was certain the attacks I had just witnessed in New York would succeed in convincing any remaining doubters that inaction was no longer an option.

Through the swirl of my emotions, I knew one other thing as well: I had to be part of my country's response. This thought was not motivated by any professional ambition, but by an urgent, all-consuming desire to do something to avenge the outrageous, murderous act I had just witnessed, and to stop it from ever happening again.

In that moment, in some deeply personal almost spiritual way, I understood that this horrific crime and my own destiny were now linked. I felt that fate had ordained that I join the CIA many years before, and that my career, and indeed perhaps my entire life, had been a preparation for this moment and for what I knew must lie ahead.

2

Plenty of Parking

After ALL THE TRAFFIC evacuating Washington cleared out, sometime after 11:00 a.m., Frank loaded the foreign delegation into the van and took them back to their hotel. It would be almost a week before they were able to get a flight back home. I don't know if they ever got their briefings on the threat of international terrorism. It didn't really matter; they had already learned the lesson.

For my part, I got in my Hyundai and drove to Langley. On the way I crossed the Roosevelt Bridge, and in the distance I could see columns of smoke rising high into the sky above the Pentagon, struck earlier by hijacked American Airlines flight 77. It was another surreal moment, and it powerfully brought home to me that war had arrived at my country's doorstep.

The traffic was light as I took the George Washington Parkway to the Route 123 exit and headed west to the entrance to CIA Headquarters. The CIA Security Police manning the entrance were in full threat regalia—submachine guns, 12 Gauge pump-action shotguns, and full body armor—clearly not the standard uniform. In my entire career I had never seen them so heavily armed. I stopped and showed them my Agency badge and was silently waved through the gate.

Turning into the southwest parking lot, I was shocked to see a sight that I'd never seen at Headquarters during a weekday—an empty parking lot close to the building! Not even on weekends had I ever seen such a deserted lot. It was then that I realized that Headquarters must have been evacuated as a precautionary measure in case the CIA compound was on al-Qa'ida's target list. Of course it made perfect sense, and I chided myself for not thinking about that before driving over. Nonetheless, I made the best of the situation and parked mere steps from the building.

I half expected to find the southwest entrance locked, but it was open and a security officer was at her post. Once through the turnstile, I made my way through deserted corridors and took the elevator up to the front office of the Near East and South Asia Division (known as the NE Division), the CIA component where I was home-based. It appeared as if the entire section was completely abandoned, but in one office I found a sole occupant—a forlorn looking, middle-aged woman named Betty who I did not recognize. I introduced myself.

"Are you an NE Division officer?" she asked.

"I am, but I've been overseas on an assignment with Counterterrorist Center for the last couple of years. I'm on leave right now but, well, after today, I'm ready to come back to work."

"Okay, I'll make a note and let the Division know. Where can we get hold of you?"

I told her we were temporarily at the Oakwood apartments until we could move into our house, and I gave her the telephone number.

"Is the Division Chief around?" I asked.

"He's with the Director right now. I don't know when he'll return."

"Alright, I'll check back tomorrow morning and see what the Division wants me to do."

"Sure," Betty said. "There really is nothing for you to do right now. Tomorrow we should know something more."

I went back to my car and drove to our apartment. Oblivious to the scenic charm of the tree-lined twists and turns of Kirby Road, images of the burning World Trade Center buildings flashed through my mind as I tried to comprehend the magnitude of the events of the morning and the horror that the victims of the attack must have experienced. That they did not deserve to die this way was the thought that kept coming to me. They were innocent. The people behind the attack had to be punished and destroyed. They were beyond any hope of redemption.

As I pulled into the parking lot, I heard on the radio that schools were being dismissed early because of the attacks. My wife was in Europe on a business trip, so responsibility for the kids on that fateful day fell to me alone. I knew by now they must have heard something about the attacks and might be upset and worried.

In the case of our daughter, who was a college sophomore at the University of Virginia, all I needed to do was to make a phone call to reassure her we were okay. Our son, however, was at a nearby middle school, and I decided to go pick him up rather than have him take the bus home. I wasn't the only parent who had made this decision, and the school parking lot was a chaotic mix of buses, cars, and kids. Out of the crowd of kids, I spotted my son standing by his bus stop. He wasn't hard to pick out. He stood taller than most of the other kids, and he was dressed in his skateboarder's ensemble: baggy pants, an oversized T-shirt, baseball cap, and a pair of Van's shoes that looked like they could have been size 14. Knowing he wouldn't be looking for me, I managed to find a spot to park and walked toward him.

"Hey, Bud!" I called.

Surprised, he turned to look at me.

"Come on. Let's go."

"Dad, what's going on? They said there's been some kind of attack with planes. What happened?"

On the way to the apartment I told him about the attacks, but I knew he would not really understand the magnitude of the situation until he saw the video of the planes hitting the Twin Towers and their terrible fall. 9/11 would be for him and his generation what the Kennedy assassination had been for mine—a shocking introduction to the awful things that men are capable of doing.

As we pulled into the Oakwood complex, it looked like most of the occupants were already home given the full parking lot, but it was eerily quiet. There was no one on the tennis courts or at the pool, and walking down the hallway of our building I didn't hear a sound. The place was like a tomb.

As all of America did, my son got his chance that day to watch the videos of the day's horrific events, probably more times than he should have, and out of concern for his mental health I eventually told him to go outside and practice on his skateboard. I think that was the only time I ever encouraged him in that particular sport.

I woke up several times that night thinking again that maybe the events of the day had only been a very bad dream. I did this for several nights, but each morning I awakened to the depressing reality of the great disaster that had struck my country.

3

Roots

The NIGHT I WAS born my father was raiding a moonshine still in the mountains of north Georgia. It is a claim few can truthfully make and to my mind it augured well for an interesting life to come. My father was largely responsible for that. Born and raised in depression-era Georgia, at age 16 and tired of picking cotton, he dropped out of school and hopped trains to California, joining the Civilian Conservation Corps (CCC). As a "pick and shovel technician" he built hiking trails along the forested northern California coast. After saving a drowning Army Sergeant, for which he received the CCC's highest decoration, he was promoted to working on the beach handing out towels and selling soft drinks.

After Pearl Harbor was bombed, Dad joined the Army. Landing at Normandy on June 10th, four days after the initial invasion, he would fight through the entire European campaign that followed. Almost captured during the Battle of the Bulge, he went on to cross the bridge at Remagen just before it collapsed. Before the war's end, he had risen to the rank of corporal—three times. This was a fact he took some delight in mentioning.

Returning home, he finally got his high school diploma and graduated from the University of Georgia, receiving a regular Army 2nd Lieutenant's commission through the ROTC program. Dad would see combat again, this time in Korea as a tank company commander, where battles resulting in 500 enemy dead were characterized as skirmishes in official reports. After Korea he resigned his commission to enter federal law enforcement as a "revenuer" raiding stills and chasing moonshiners on the twisting back roads of the north Georgia mountains; hence, his absence on my birth night.

Afterward, Dad transferred to the U.S. Forest Service as a criminal investigator, and the family moved to a rural community in the Rio Grande valley south of Albuquerque. I spent my formative years there among the cottonwood trees and alfalfa fields crisscrossed by irrigation canals and barbed-wire fences. All of this watched over by the ever-present Manzano Mountains that stood blue and purple on the distant horizon.

At one point we had eleven horses, two milk cows, a good bird dog named Kate, and an occasional pig or two, no names assigned. Much of my daily routine revolved around keeping those animals fed and watered, and in the case of the cows, emptied of milk twice a day, every day.

For fun, in addition to riding those horses, three of which we had broken and trained ourselves over the course of a summer, my other past time was playing Army, imagining I was fighting the enemies my father had once fought. I also loved hunting, particularly the fast action that followed the flush of a covey of desert quail that Kate had pointed. But the big event was elk hunting in the Pecos Wilderness in northern New Mexico when we would pack into the mountains on horseback and set up a base camp from which we forayed early each morning into the yellow-leafed aspen forests of mid-autumn in search of bull elk.

There were other adventures as well. Once, our family was taken into federal protective custody when my father's life was threatened by a man named Reyes Lopez Tijerina. He was the leader of a militant organization called the "Alianza." Dad had arrested Tijerina in a tense, guns drawn, high-noon style showdown during the late 1960s land grant wars of northern New Mexico. Another time, Dad equipped my cousin and me with a camera to surreptitiously take photos of a jeep club that was illegally driving in the vehicle-restricted Gila Wilderness in southern New Mexico. Using the cover of trout fishing in the rushing cold waters of the Gila River, we snapped the incriminating photos and a successful legal case was made against the jeep club.

When I think of all the experiences I had growing up, I cannot imagine a better boyhood than the one I had, and at times I have felt bad that I could not give my own son and daughter the same experiences which my father, with my mother's loving assistance, gave to me.

My father would eventually rise in his career to the position of National Director for Law Enforcement, the most senior law enforcement position in the U.S. Forest Service. Not bad for a high school dropout and twice busted Army corporal. A soft-spoken, easygoing man, he never directly told me what I should do with my life, but his influence on me was powerful nonetheless.

My long-term career intention was to work in federal law enforcement, and I majored in Police Science toward that end. No doubt because of my father's example, however, I believed I had an obligation to serve my country in the military. I obtained a regular Army commission through the ROTC program at New Mexico State University, and subsequently served six years of active duty.

My troop unit service was with what at the time were called Rapid Deployment units, in my case, the 82nd Airborne Division and the 7th Special Forces Group, which I had wanted to join since reading *The Green Berets* by Robin Moore when I was a kid. I believed that if there was a conflict it was likely I would be deployed. As it happened, with the exception of the Granada action and the invasion of Panama, neither in which I participated, my Army years were during peacetime and I spent my time training for a contingency that never arose. I left the Army thinking I had gotten off lightly, particularly in comparison to my father who had spent years of his life at war, and then spent the rest of his life having nightmares about it.

Once I decided to leave the Army, it was my father who pointed out a CIA recruitment advertisement in the *Army Times* and suggested I might want to apply. I had not really considered the Agency for a career, believing that I would probably need to speak a foreign language and have a Master's degree, neither of which turned out to be a requirement. I applied, and to my amazement, was hired and became an operations officer, also known as a "case officer" in the CIA's Directorate of Operations, or D.O.

On 10 September 2001, I was 45 years old and married with two kids. I had completed multiple, traditional CIA tours overseas and at Headquarters, and I had been out of the Army for almost 18 years. The last thing I would have imagined was that I might soon be headed into a war zone.

4

A Day Late

In THE FIRST DAYS following the 9/11 attacks, I spent my time at Headquarters trying to join whatever office would head up CIA's response. That proved to be harder than I'd thought it would be.

In the immediate aftermath of the attacks, it was unclear which office would be given the lead responsibility for CIA's role: NE Division or the Counterterrorist Center, known as CTC. NE's area of responsibility included the Taliban-ruled country of Afghanistan that served as al-Qa'ida's sanctuary. This meant that NE owned the turf, in terms of the U.S. intelligence interests and operations there. CTC, on the other hand, had no territorial responsibilities, but was charged with the worldwide counterterrorist mission. Not knowing which office would take the lead, I hedged my bets by staying on leave status for several days, even as I walked the sterile corridors of Headquarters trying to learn as much as I could about what was happening.

Soon I heard that CTC would be in charge and had already organized a team that would be deploying to Afghanistan. The CTC team's mission was to link up with the Northern Alliance, an Afghan organization made up of Tajik, Uzbek, Turkmen, and Hazara minorities that had been fighting the Pashtun Taliban for years. Importantly, the Northern Alliance was the only organized anti-Taliban force that held territory in Afghanistan. The CIA team, whose formal designation was the Northern Alliance Liaison Team (NALT), code-named "JAWBREAKER," would be led by Gary Schroen, a highly experienced and decorated operations officer. Gary was in the agency's retirement transition program on 9/11, but given his relevant and much needed experience, he was asked to delay his retirement in order to lead the NALT. Gary readily accepted the dangerous assignment.

CIA was not a stranger to the Northern Alliance, having maintained contact with the organization for years. During that time, CIA teams had made trips inside Afghanistan to keep up the liaison contact. Complicating Gary's task, however, was the recent assassination of Ahmad Shah Masood, the Northern Alliance's charismatic and legendary military leader, who was killed only days before the 9/11 attacks by a suicide al-Qa'ida team posing as journalists. With Masood gone, it was not clear how the Northern Alliance would be impacted in its ability to continue the fight against the Taliban.

The NALT's mission was especially critical as it was the first step of the U.S. strategy developed by CTC under the leadership of Cofer Black. Importantly, in keeping with the Bush Administration's preference, the strategy avoided the use of conventional U.S. ground forces. Instead, it called for small, combined teams of CIA and U.S. Special Forces personnel to deploy to Afghanistan to work directly with the Northern Alliance forces, as well as other armed Afghan groups. Their mission would be to locate and destroy al-Qa'ida, and as necessary, Taliban forces. A major component of the plan would be U.S. air power that would be used to attack strategic enemy targets and provide close air support to the friendly Afghan fighters acting as the surrogate maneuver forces on the ground.

After I heard about the formation of the NALT, I talked to NE Division management and obtained their agreement that I could stay on with CTC for the next several months. I immediately set out to find Gary Schroen to let him know I was available and would like to join his team. It took me a couple of days to run him down, as he proved to be a moving target, busy as he was trying to put his team together and make the necessary preparations for deploying.

I knew Gary from earlier in my career but not particularly well, and I had never worked directly with him. I really wasn't sure he would even remember me. I decided that, if presented with the opportunity, I had to make a good case for why he should take me with him. Finally, purely by chance, I ran into him at the NE Division front office.

"Hi, Gary. I understand you're putting together a team to deploy to Afghanistan."

"Yeah, Duane, how are you doing?

Well, at least he remembers me, I thought.

"I'm finalizing the arrangements right now," he continued.

"If it's not too late, I'd like to join your team. I just came back from a COS position with CTC, and I'm available to deploy. I'm a former Army Special Forces officer and I speak Farsi."

I figured my military background, although admittedly dated, would be valuable given the team's destination and mission, so I made sure Gary knew about it. I also threw in the part about speaking Farsi as he himself was a Farsi speaker, and the Persian Farsi was similar to the Dari spoken in parts of Afghanistan.

Gary looked at me for a second.

"Well, it's not clear when we're going to leave, but it could be any day. I've got a meeting right now, but let me check into it. I'll get back to you tomorrow."

Although my encounter with Gary was brief, my goal was accomplished, and the next day I met with him again. The news was positive.

"You better start getting some gear together ASAP. Things are moving quickly and there's a good chance we'll leave very soon."

It looked like I was going to get what I had asked for, but with possibly just a day or two to prepare there was very little time to get myself organized. The family and I were still living out of suitcases in a temporary apartment, and I had no gear or clothing with me that would be suitable for the environment and the mission. Gary had said I should go out and buy what I needed, as the Agency had no clothing or gear to issue me at Headquarters.

The only good thing about the timing of all this was that my wife, who had been stranded in Europe for several days trying to get a flight home, was finally back and she could take the lead in running the household so I could focus on getting ready for imminent deployment.

But my worrying about how I would get everything together in such a short time was wasted energy. It turned out the team's departure had suddenly been moved up and on 19 September, the same day that Gary and I had last talked, the team left—without me.

Too late in my effort to join Gary's team, my only alternative was to join the office that would oversee the Afghanistan effort and then try to get on another team. After a couple of false leads as to the office's location, I finally was directed to a suite in the New Headquarters Building. At first I thought the place was deserted, but then I found a little corner office with three people sitting in it. I introduced myself to a clear-eyed man of bearish stature who, because he sat behind the only desk, seemed to be in charge. His name was Frank, and he told me I had come to the right place.

With a sweep of his hand he said, "This is CTC/Special Operations, and we're going take the war to al-Qa'ida."

I glanced over at the only other people around, a man and woman who did not appear to be doing much of anything at the moment, and said, "Well, it sure looks like you could use a little more help."

Frank laughed, "Oh yeah, we're just getting started. Hank Crumpton has just been selected to be our chief, and he's still en route from overseas. Other than Joanne and John here, and a few stray dogs and cats, this is all the staff we have for the moment."

"How do I sign on?"

"Well, we're looking for qualified volunteers, but this is going to be a different kind of mission than the D.O. typically takes on. Hank has said we'll vet everyone before official acceptance. I'll have to review your file and confer with him when he gets to Washington. Then, I'll let you know."

I knew Hank already. He had been one of my Headquarters overseers while I was a COS in Latin America. I was glad to hear he would be in charge. When it came to CT operations, he was deadly serious. In fact he had been pushing for a much more aggressive policy against al-Qa'ida long before 9/11. I figured this was why he had been chosen to head up the CIA's response to the attacks.

"Sounds like a plan," I said. "I'm not sure who is holding my personnel file right now, CTC or NE."

"Don't worry. We can track it down."

Frank jotted down his secure number on a post-it and handed it to me.

"Check back with me in a couple of days."

In two days I called him. He apologized, saying he had been unable to lay his hands on my file. Apparently neither CTC nor NE could find it.

"I'll see if I can run it down," I told him.

My efforts were also futile. My file was nowhere to be found, and I was starting to get more than a little frustrated. I knew time was of the essence. I had already missed being part of Gary's team, and now, because my file had apparently fallen in a large crack between CTC and NE, I was wasting my time walking the halls of Headquarters. *This should not be this hard*, I thought to myself.

A day or two later, I ran into Frank. "Hey, I was just about to call you. Forget about looking for your file," he said. "Hank is here, and I ran your name past him. You're in. Welcome to CTC/SO."

5

A Threshold Crossed,
A Spark Ignited

The ATTACKS ON SEPTEMBER 11, 2001 were not the first time a terrorist act had captured my undivided attention. That distinction, that first entering into my consciousness of terrorism as a phenomenon, occurred in the late summer of 1972 when I was between my sophomore and junior years of high school. My father had just been transferred from New Mexico to Washington, D.C., and we were temporarily living in the Breezeway Motel in Fairfax while we looked for a house.

This was not a happy time in my life. I had just left a state I loved and all the friends I had ever known. I was dreading the idea of starting a new school where I didn't know a soul. The only thing that gave me any solace was the hope that if I could only make it through the next two years—which seemed like an eternity then—when I graduated, I would return to New Mexico and attend college.

My feelings of loneliness and gloom were only made worse when our much loved black and tan miniature dachshund, "Smoochy," succumbed from wounds received after being mauled by a pack of large dogs. The fact that Smoochy, whose courage far exceeded his physical abilities, had caused the incident by charging into the dogs, believing he was defending his owners, provided little comfort.

During those melancholy days the Summer Olympics were taking place in Munich, Germany, and I spent many an hour in our small hotel room watching the various competitions, grateful for the diversion. When the first news reports began to break that something was amiss at the Olympic Village, I was immediately drawn into the developing story. Soon the world learned that Israeli athletes had been attacked and were being held hostage. The armed hostage-takers were radical Palestinians from a group known as "Black September." They were making pronouncements and demands that, if not met, would result in the death of the hostages.

I was shocked by what was happening. Who were these people, these "Black September" radicals? Did they seriously think they were going to accomplish their goals? And did they really believe they were going to get away with it? It seemed crazy. At times, one of the hostage-takers would even brazenly step out in the open on an apartment balcony, his head covered by a ski mask, seemingly unconcerned about being shot. Was he nuts?

The audacity of the attack was mind-blowing to me. It contravened what I knew or had assumed about how people were supposed to behave. This was the Olympics after all. Countries and the people of the world were supposed to come together in peace, putting aside their differences in pursuit of athletic competition. What was going on?

As the events unfolded I remained glued to the drama, following it to the bitter and tragic end. I did not go to bed, as the rest of my family did, when the late night TV news reported that the hostages were safely rescued by police and the radicals were dead. For some reason I doubted that this rosy outcome was true, and I stayed up waiting for more details. Later, when an accurate report did come, the news was terrible. Not only were the hostages not safe, they were all dead—eleven in total. Five of the eight Palestinians were killed and three captured.* As the news sank in, I sensed that a threshold had been crossed, that the rules of civilization that previously existed no longer did. The doors of the world had been opened to whatever evil desired to walk through, and I was gripped by a sense of foreboding. I'm certain this feeling was magnified by the general malaise I was already experiencing. Even so, after all these years, that same feeling surfaces each time a major terrorist incident occurs.

---

*The three captured Black September members would be traded a short time later as part of an exchange for a hijacked airliner and its passengers and crew.

The 1972 attack at the Olympics was a catalyst for me. It sparked a serious interest in international affairs and national security issues, including terrorism, which I continued to follow as I progressed through high school and college. My commissioning into the Military Intelligence branch of the Army after college enabled me to follow these interests in a professional realm. By the time I had entered the Army in the late '70s, counterterrorism was evolving into a more formalized field. Within the Army the premiere counterterrorism element, popularly known as "Delta Force," had formed and was actively recruiting from the ranks.

At the time I was serving as a platoon leader in the 82nd Airborne Division at Ft. Bragg, North Carolina, and I was envious when one of my battalion's company commanders successfully made it through the selection program for Delta. I was interested in joining the force myself because special operations and the counterterrorist mission had great appeal to me. I was already Ranger-qualified having attended Ranger school as an ROTC cadet, so I thought that might count for something. But after checking with the unit's recruiters, my hopes were crushed. I was told because I was only a lieutenant and had not completed my advanced branch course, nor served as a company commander, I was ineligible to apply.

I was eligible, however, for Special Forces, commonly known as the "Green Berets." At that time, Special Forces was not its own branch within the Army and assignment was on a "branch immaterial" basis, meaning it didn't matter if you were an infantryman or a mechanic, as long as you could pass the SF qualification course you were in. So in late summer of 1980 I transferred from the 82nd Airborne to 7th Special Forces Group located in the Smoke Bomb Hill area of Ft. Bragg. In September I began the SF Officer's Qualification Course and graduated in December. Although not the Army's dedicated counterterrorist element, as a direct action-capable force, CT operations were still part of the SF mission, and some of the unit training and specialized courses were directly relevant to that mission. Given this, my Special Forces tour helped to advance my understanding of counterterrorism at a tactical level.

In 1982, I received orders for an assignment as an instructor to the Army's Intelligence Center and School at Fort Huachuca, Arizona. This historic cavalry post, located in the southeastern corner of the state, is where the great Apache chief, Cochise, had once roamed. Although glad to be returning to the Southwest, I left Special Forces with misgivings, but had little choice at the time. I knew my officer status meant I would likely only have one more SF assignment in my career, and only then if I was lucky. In future years Special Forces would become a branch unto itself, allowing officers to spend much of their careers in SF-related assignments, but that change occurred after I had left the Army.

In addition to being in the Southwest, another positive point of my new assignment was that one of the courses I would teach was intelligence support in low-intensity conflict, a topic that included terrorism. This teaching responsibility allowed me to deepen my knowledge and understanding of terrorism through research and working with others knowledgeable in the field.

It was during this assignment that I made the decision to leave the Army. I had already been in for over five years, which was longer than I had intended. I still aspired to a career in federal law enforcement, and I applied to the FBI and DEA. At my father's suggestion I also applied to the CIA. Although not a law enforcement agency, Dad thought it might be a good fit for me, and the more I thought about it, the more it seemed like it might be an interesting place to work. The CIA was the first to process my application, and in less than a year I was accepted for employment.

I knew the experience I gained from the Army would benefit me in many ways in the coming years at the CIA. What I didn't know was just how well, seemingly tailor-made, that experience combined with my training and years of operational work at the CIA, would prepare me for when I would join the ranks of CTC/Special Operations.

6

Mission Over Process

Following THE 9/11 ATTACKS I signed off from leave status and officially reported for duty during the third week of September. By this time, more people were being assigned, and CTC/SO had moved to a larger office at CIA Headquarters. There were none of the typical cubicles; instead, tables set up end-to-end and topped with desktop computers formed a large rectangle in the center of the room. It was an unusual arrangement, but it was the most expeditious way to get a new office up and running. Also expedited was the process for getting the necessary computer access. This process normally could take a week or more when someone new joined an office. In the case of CTC/SO, I had all my access in less than 20 minutes. It was a simple but elegant example of mission taking priority over process. During my tenure with CTC/SO, it would become apparent that this was the rule, rather than the exception. In my view, it was this principle more than anything else that made CTC/SO such a successful counterterrorist organization.

Our mission statement was straightforward and unambiguous: destroy al-Qa'ida. Accomplishing that mission, however, was not so straightforward. For the moment, al-Qa'ida was in Afghanistan protected by the Taliban government and its troops. To destroy it, we needed the Taliban to either help us or get out of our way. If ongoing diplomatic efforts did not succeed in obtaining the Taliban's agreement to choose one of those options, then we would have to go through them to get to al-Qa'ida. No one where I was sitting expected the Taliban to cooperate with the United States, and our planning proceeded accordingly.

It was only after I was briefed-in at CTC/SO that I fully understood the central role CIA was to have in the war in Afghanistan, and why. A major reason was the Bush Administration's decision not to respond to the 9/11 attacks with conventional ground forces, fearing that if it did, the U.S. would be repeating the same mistake made by the Soviet Union when it invaded Afghanistan in 1979, when disastrous consequences accrued. Instead, the administration chose to employ covert resources and methods. This meant that CIA, which had the responsibility for executing covert action, would take the lead role. It also meant that the legal framework underpinning the effort, namely Title 50 of the U.S. legal code, which governs intelligence activities and covert action, would provide the authority for CIA to take action against al-Qa'ida. Had the Administration initially pursued a conventional military option, then Title 10, which governs U.S. military operations, would have applied, and CIA's role would have been less central, though still important.

Because of these circumstances, it was the CIA that had developed the war strategy. CIA would also provide the means to carry it out by enlisting the support of anti-Taliban Afghan forces with whom the Agency already maintained relationships. Depending on need, new relationships could be established as well. Since U.S. conventional ground forces were not to be used, our success in Afghanistan would rest almost entirely on CIA's ability to get these anti-Taliban forces to fight the ground war for us. That was the hinge on which everything else would swing.

Despite the expansive role that CIA, and in particular CTC/SO, would play in the overall U.S. effort, at that early juncture the focus of CTC/SO was to support the Northern Alliance Liaison Team, even as plans for deploying additional teams were being made. To this end, Hank Crumpton's standing order was whatever the NALT needed, it would get. If it didn't, there would be hell to pay.

One incident that drove this home occurred only a couple of days after Hank assumed control. Early one evening, a cable from the NALT arrived at Headquarters requesting a planeload of supplies be air dropped to the Northern Alliance. In addition to the normal coordination required in tasking and moving an aircraft internationally, the request would require a CIA logistics base in Europe to obtain and organize the supplies for delivery. The following morning at the 0700 staff meeting, Hank asked the chief of logistics if the supplies had been delivered. When the officer replied that the request had only come in less than 12 hours earlier, Hank exploded in a thunderous rage.

"I don't give a flying fuck when the request came in! I want those supplies there now!"

All of us were taken aback by the fury Hank unleashed on the logs chief. Everyone at the table, Hank included I believe, knew it would have been an impossible task to deliver the tons of supplies overnight. Still, it put everyone on notice that the impossible was exactly what we were expected to deliver.

7

Change Comes Hard

One OF THE FIRST tasks CTC/SO faced was to identify more people that could be brought into the effort. I immediately began to reach out to officers who would be good additions to the team. Those who were former military and spoke Farsi, Dari, or Pashto were obvious choices, but in truth, there weren't many of them to be found. The less than a handful with this combination of skills and background whom I knew were already serving at overseas stations; it would require the agreement of their station chiefs and their divisions to release them for service with CTC/SO. Much to my dismay, obtaining their release turned out to be more problematic than I thought it would be. Despite the unique and critical skills these officers had and how badly we needed them for the mission we faced, a surprising—and in my opinion—disappointing number of supervisors resisted having their officers reassigned. Instead these managers chose to act as if it was still business as usual. Given the crisis we faced, I saw this as a failure of leadership, an area where CIA had a mixed record.

My training at the CIA to become a Directorate of Operations (D.O.) case officer in the early 1980's did not include leadership training. It was the height of the Cold War, and CIA training was focused only on how to run intelligence operations, i.e. spotting, assessing, developing, recruiting, handling, and terminating human intelligence sources. It was great training for this skill set, and I fully understood how to do the job of a case officer once through with the training. But if the CIA training had been my only professional training or experience, I would have had little understanding of leadership principles, styles, and methods, and their importance to an organization and mission accomplishment.

The lack of training or emphasis on leadership as a subject or practice within the D.O. was a revelation and a disappointment for me when I first came to the Agency, particularly having just left the Army where emphasis on leadership was constant and expected to be exhibited at all times, no matter a soldier's rank. But at the time I entered on duty with the Agency, there were only a couple of leadership courses, and they were only available for a select number of fairly senior-level officers. For some of them, in my opinion anyway, it came too late in their professional development to make a positive impact on them or the CIA. But for the broad swath of officers going through the early to mid-part of their careers, there was a huge void in their preparation to become leaders. For at least the first 15 years of my CIA career I don't think I ever heard a significant conversation about leadership in the hallways or offices at Langley or overseas stations. It just wasn't something that was considered important. The assumption seemed to be that if you had the skills to do your job, that was really all you needed. What this resulted in were too many people being placed in leadership or management positions who were unprepared to manage, motivate, and lead people in accomplishing the mission of the CIA. This is not to say, there were no good leaders. In fact, there were many excellent ones, but the percentage of bad leaders was too high, and it negatively impacted the morale of the work force and ultimately the mission.

Fortunately toward the end of my career, the Agency's attitude about leadership began to change, and more training was developed and made available to employees at all levels. Some of it was very good training and addressed both leadership and teamwork, and my sense of things when I left was that it was beginning to make a positive difference for the organization, particularly in terms of employees' morale. However, this change in organizational culture and the emphasis on leadership and teamwork would come largely after the 9/11 attacks.

In September 2001, however, even knowing the Agency's culture toward leadership, it was still beyond my comprehension how any CIA officer could have the attitude I was witnessing, even as the daily news showed scenes of the devastation in New York, at the Pentagon, and in Pennsylvania.

I had experienced a form of this attitude firsthand several days after the attacks while I was still trying to join CTC/SO. I had stopped by the office of a senior level NE Division officer that I knew and with whom I had served overseas. I told him that I was trying to get on one of the teams going to Afghanistan.

"I wouldn't advise it," he said. "Those teams are made up of paramilitary officers. You're not a paramilitary officer, you're a case officer. You won't be doing traditional operations officer work that promotion panels will be looking for. Going to Afghanistan won't do anything for your career."

I was shocked by his comment, disgusted really. The truth was, I had not even thought about my career from the moment I had seen the World Trade Center towers collapse. The idea of "career" to be mentioned in this context struck me as repugnant.

Another officer I talked to also could not understand why I would want to go to Afghanistan, but his lack of understanding had nothing to do with career, but family.

"How could you do that to your family? You've got a wife and kids? What if something happens to you?"

It was a good question. There was nothing more important to me than my family. Throughout my career I had always weighed the pluses and minuses of potential assignments with my family in mind, striving for a rough balance that would allow me to do interesting work that contributed to my country's security, yet one in which my family would be safe and able to have things like a reasonable place to live, good schools, and a good community. I had been lucky, as most of my assignments had met those requirements, but my very first overseas tour had proven to be exceptionally difficult, even disastrous, due to issues well beyond my control, and it negatively affected both me and my family.

After that first tour, hoping for a more "normal" overseas assignment I had accepted a job in the Middle East at a location well known to be a great family post with good schools and housing, and a stable political environment.

Just prior to our departure to the new post, however, the first Gulf war broke out. I was instructed to delay our departure and to stay in Washington. Having already moved out of our house, we began living out of suitcases in a temporary, furnished apartment in Arlington while my daughter started a new, temporary school. At the same time, my three-year-old son was having a difficult time adjusting to all the changes. Then to top things off, my wife suffered a debilitating injury. It was not the best of times, but at least I was there to help out. When the Gulf war ended, I was told I could report to post, but the assignment would be "unaccompanied," meaning my family would have to stay behind. I knew I would be leaving them in a bad situation.

After much soul-searching, I requested to have my assignment curtailed. It was the hardest decision I think I ever made during my career, but it all boiled down to one thing—at that moment in time my family needed me more than the Agency did. I paid a price for the curtailment in terms of career advancement, and perhaps most painful to me, damage to my reputation from those who only knew part of the story. But it was a price I was ready to pay and I never regretted it.

But in the case of going to Afghanistan, the shoe was now on the other foot. My family's situation was stable compared to many years before, but my country's situation wasn't. This time the Agency needed me more than my family did. Getting on a team going to Afghanistan was the right thing for me to do. In fact, as far as I was concerned, it was the only thing for me to do.

Unfortunately, while I worked to make that happen, I found the attitude that "this whole terrorism thing will pass if we just wait long enough," was more prevalent than I would have believed. With the 9/11 attacks, the world had changed, and the mission of the CIA had to change as well. But somehow, a significant number of otherwise smart and dedicated officers just did not see it that way.

While this attitude was a disappointment for me, what made up for it were the many other officers from throughout the CIA who were doing whatever they could to support the effort to strike back hard. It soon became obvious to me that CTC/SO was comprised entirely of those kinds of officers.

For me, however, serving in CTC/SO at Headquarters was not what I wanted. Although it was an important job, I did not like deskwork and never thought of myself as being particularly good at it. I believed that with my temperament and the various skills and abilities I possessed, I would be of better use in the field. But the challenge I faced in getting on one of the teams bound for Afghanistan was pretty straightforward: I was a case officer and—as my NE colleague had pointed out—the teams were almost entirely made up of CIA paramilitary officers drawn from the Special Activities Division, or SAD.

In the case of paramilitary officers, there was no question about them joining the fight in Afghanistan. Carrying out this type of mission was their *raison d'être*. All were former military, often recruited into CIA from one of the military's special operations units such as the Army's Delta Force or the Navy's SEALs. By any standard they were the *crème-de-la-crème* of the military prior to being recruited by the CIA. Most had also been cross-trained as CIA operations officers, meaning they not only had valuable military hard skills, they also knew how to recruit and handle agents and report intelligence, the bread and butter tasks of a field case officer. In short, they possessed the perfect hybrid of skills for service in Afghanistan.

As for my chance of deploying on a team, all I could do at this point was to keep my fingers crossed.

8

"Pasha"

As THE DAYS PASSED, more and more officers showed up for duty at CTC/SO and took their seats at the computers to read-in. One of the team's first priorities was to coordinate with the Department of Defense for the quick deployment of a Special Forces Operational Detachment Alpha, or "ODA"—also referred to as an "A"-Team—to join the NALT in Afghanistan's Panjshir Valley. ODA's would also be needed to partner with other CIA teams that were deploying in the coming weeks. To everyone's dismay, however, due to various complications within DOD, it would not be until after mid-October that the first Special Forces ODA would be on the ground in Afghanistan with the NALT.

From late September to late October much of CTC/SO's work dealt with logistics, planning, and coordination with various military headquarters as well as the State Department and the National Security Council. At the same time, the office was responsible for tracking what was happening on the ground and providing daily intelligence briefings and situational updates to Agency leadership on the 7th floor and to the White House. I had no specific responsibilities related to those tasks, but I pitched in whenever I saw something I could do, such as answer a cable or coordinate with another office on some issue. It wasn't exciting work, but I was at least making a contribution, even if a small one, while I waited to be assigned to a team.

One day I received a call from a desk officer in NE Division who had information on an Afghan who had formerly been a CIA reporting source. Because his access had shifted away from what CIA was most interested in, to international narcotics trafficking, he had been turned over to the Drug Enforcement Administration a couple of years before. The desk officer said the source, who was informally referred to as "Pasha," was currently in the U.S. and, in light of the 9/11 attacks, DEA thought he might be of use to CIA again.

In describing the source to me, the desk officer mentioned that Pasha was from a remote province in northern Afghanistan, a place where we believed Osama Bin Laden might flee once our efforts in Afghanistan got fully underway. We had no sources in that province, and Pasha was well connected there. If we could get him to return home and tap into his network, there was a reasonable chance he might pick up on any al-Qa'ida moving into the area. Pasha sounded like an interesting operational lead, and I made arrangements to meet him at a hotel in the next couple of days.

Accompanying me to meet with Pasha was a retired case officer named Joan who, following the 9/11 attacks, had immediately volunteered to come back to work and help out wherever she could. Well into her sixties, Joan had been enjoying her retirement writing children's books, but had put that love aside to return to serve her country in its time of need. She brought with her a great personality and a great deal of operational experience; CTC/SO was fortunate to have her services. During her career she had served in the Near East region and at one point had been a Chief of Station. She and I hit it off immediately, and with management's approval we teamed up to evaluate Pasha's potential operational usefulness.

We departed CIA Headquarters and after taking the necessary precautions to insure that we were not being followed, arrived at a local hotel where the meeting was to take place. The suite for the meeting had already been reserved, and I checked in using an alias. For purposes of dealing with Pasha, I was "Ian" and Joan used the throwaway alias of "Elaine."

The meeting with Pasha was a "cold turnover," meaning his current handler from DEA would not be there to make the introduction. We would have to introduce ourselves without the benefit of an interlocutor. This was not the best way to do a turnover, but sometimes it was the only way it could be done.

Shortly after our arrival and right on schedule, Pasha called from the lobby and asked for "Mr. Ian." I told him the room number and a few minutes later he knocked on the door. Pasha was thick-set and imposing. With a stern expression and jet black hair and beard, with eyes to match, he presented the stereotypical image of a Middle Eastern terrorist. I imagined the attention he must have been receiving since the 9/11 attacks, and in fact, the attention Pasha's looks drew would present some challenges for us in the coming days.

After introductions and offerings of tea, I began a debriefing of Pasha, asking him questions about where he was from and whom he knew back home. Pasha's native language was Dari, the Afghan dialect of Farsi, but his English was better than my Farsi, so I carried out the debriefing in English.

Pasha appeared to be forthcoming, and it was obvious he was used to being debriefed. I had already read his file from when he was a source for CIA, so I knew quite a bit about him. As we had planned ahead of time, during the debriefing Joan did not ask questions but played the role of my "assistant." This allowed her to carefully observe Pasha and take detailed notes.

Pasha's demeanor was serious, but his politeness and reserved manner were appealing. Still, he did have significant personal baggage, which I knew about from his file, and it was anything but appealing; there were many detractors of the case. Despite this, however, due to his access to intelligence, Pasha was kept on the books.

Finally, I introduced the subject I really wanted to discuss.

"Pasha, what do you think? Do you believe bin Laden is still in Afghanistan?"

"Yes, he is still in Afghanistan, but he no doubt has gone into deep hiding. He is not stupid. He knows America is looking for him and will kill him if he is found."

"Is there any reason to think he or other al-Qa'ida members might show up in your home province?"

"That is a possibility," Pasha said. "A few years back, some al-Qa'ida men came through the province. They were looking into acquiring mining interests in the area. I heard they made some deals and those mines could be excellent hideouts."

Pasha then leaned toward me and in a lowered voice said, "And do not forget, Mr. Ian, the border with Pakistan is not far from there. It will be their escape route should things become too uncomfortable for them in Afghanistan."

Nothing Pasha had said was new or original, nor was I expecting it to be. We already knew about al-Qa'ida's interest in mines. The group relied on the sale of semi-precious stones like Lapis Lazuli, the deep blue stones for which Afghanistan was famous, to help generate income to finance its activities. Also, there had been speculation that the mines could serve as cover for creating secret bunkers where men and material could be hidden. As for the proximity of the province to the Pakistan border and the likelihood of it serving as a back door for bin Laden's escape, that was as obvious as the rather broad nose on Pasha's tough-looking face. All you needed to do was look at a map to figure that out.

No, there was nothing in the conversation that CIA did not already know or had not considered. But the discussion did serve my purpose, as it let Pasha explain the very rationale I would use to convince him why it was important for him to go back to his province and reestablish his information network. Of course there would be a cost for his services, but in the interest of establishing a picket line of reporting sources in a remote area where bin Laden and his cronies might flee, CIA was ready to pay a premium.

"Pasha, you would make a great analyst," I said. "Your thinking is the same as the combined brain power of the CIA." Pasha beamed.

"We are very worried that the people in al-Qa'ida, maybe bin Laden himself, will slip away before we can catch them. Your province, because of all the things you mentioned, could be the place that will swallow them up and bin Laden may never be seen again. That cannot be allowed to happen. He has committed a terrible crime, and he must be punished for it."

As I talked, Pasha sat very still. His face had a stern look about it, and he seemed intently focused on my every word. When I stopped, he continued to sit motionless for several seconds. Then he smiled.

"So, Mr. Ian, what must I do?"

"We need you to go back to your home province and reestablish your reporting network. This time we want you to be watching for al-Qa'ida, not narcotics traffickers."

I stopped to watch his reaction as Joan quietly scribbled some notes.

"I will need money to do this. Maybe a lot of money," Pasha said.

Now it was his turn to carefully watch my reaction. His words were not unexpected. In my experience as a case officer, most agents seemed to have been programmed to respond in this manner when given a new tasking.

"You will get the money you need for this, and a nice boost in your salary. Possibly a bonus as well—if you are successful. But first you need to prepare a plan on how you would go about making this happen. How would you get there? What would you tell your friends and family you were doing? Who would you use as sources, and how would you stay in contact with them? I'll need timelines for getting everything in place. Everything you can think of, including how much money you think you'll need. Once you've done that, we'll sit down and go over the plan top to bottom and fix any problems. Can you do all that?"

"No problem, Mr. Ian. I can do this for you, and CIA will be very happy. I know how to make this work."

"I know you do, Pasha. That is why we wanted to meet you again. We know we can depend on you to get this done."

In preparation for the meeting, Joan and I had pulled together maps and ordered special photography of selected areas of his province. The photography was an Air Force product that presented the terrain in a 3D format similar to what it would look like if you were flying through the area. The terrain we were interested in was unbelievably rugged, with narrow valleys and gorges that were bordered on each side by the exceptionally steep mountains of the Hindu Kush. If Bin Laden wanted to hide there it would be very difficult, perhaps impossible, to find him. The best chance we had would be to detect his initial movement into the area, and to do that we needed a local source network. That was what we hoped Pasha could provide.

As the meeting continued, Joan and I spread out the terrain map on the table. Unlike most assets from the Third World I had worked with, Pasha could easily read a map, and he quickly pointed out his home village. There were few roads in the area, and Pasha confirmed that much travel was done using trails not shown on the map.

"It's easy to know where the trails are," he said. "Almost every valley that is big enough for a stream or river will have a trail running near it."

"And what about crossing from one valley to the next? How is that done?" Joan asked, momentarily breaking from her role as note-taker. "Those mountainsides are very steep."

"Yes, very steep. But there is always a way." Pasha flashed a grin through his black beard. "But it may take several days to make the crossing. And in winter, forget it. You're not going anywhere. The snow is just too deep, and the passes are closed."

"So what do you do in the winter?" I asked.

"Not much. You spend almost all your time inside your compound trying to stay warm. Your supplies have been stored by the time winter begins, and you keep your animals in your compound with you. So there really is not much need to go outside, even if you could."

"So if al-Qa'ida is there in the winter, they won't be moving about?"

Pasha shook his head. "Nobody moves in winter. Everyone will be sheltered, or they won't last long."

The discussion with Pasha made it abundantly clear that if we hoped to find our quarry, it would have to be done before winter set in. It was already October and I had serious doubts that it could be done in time. If we were going to have any chance at all, we would have to work fast.

9

Suspicious Minds

Over THE COURSE OF the next couple of weeks Joan and I had a few more hotel meetings with Pasha to review his plan for how he would return to Afghanistan and set up his source network. We also needed to train him on how to use a GPS device. This would be a critical skill for him, and one he would have to know well enough that he could also train members of his network. By using the GPS, the locations of any al-Qaida members could be accurately determined and reported back for targeting purposes. From my college ROTC days when I competed in the sport of orienteering, and from my six years in the Army that included Ranger School and the Special Forces Qualification course, I knew how to use a map and compass very well. But my Army service pre-dated GPS technology, so I was in no position to train anyone on it. For this task, SAD provided a young paramilitary officer named Ted to assist us.

After briefing Ted on the case, we arranged to pick up Pasha and take him to a large park in northern Virginia where we would conduct the training. It was the weekend and the weather was nice that day, so there were quite a few people at the park. If there had been more time, we would have preferred to do the training on a military base or at a CIA facility, but it wasn't possible to make those arrangements in the short timeframe we had; the park would have to do. The problem was, with the memory of 9/11 still very fresh in everyone's mind, Pasha's pronounced Afghan appearance and ethnic style of clothing immediately attracted the attention of anyone who saw him. The fact we were working with a GPS only heightened people's interest and suspicion.

"This isn't good. We've got to get away from all these people. I wouldn't be surprised if they called the cops on us," I said.

Ted agreed. We finally found an area of the park where there wasn't anyone around, and we were able to complete the training in a couple of hours. I took advantage of Ted's instructions as well, knowing that if I ever made it to Afghanistan I would need to know how to use the GPS.

As we made our way back to the parking area and began to encounter more people, Pasha once again began to draw attention. We got in the car, and as we pulled away, I saw in the rear view mirror a middle-aged man with his two children by his side, writing down our license plate number. I wasn't worried that he might call in the plate number to the police or the FBI because I had an Agency credential I could produce if need be. What did worry me, though, was how much attention Pasha drew to himself simply by the way he looked. I imagined the kind of attention he would generate from both the public and airport security personnel when he went to Dulles Airport in a few days holding a ticket with Pakistan as his destination. If he or his luggage were subjected to extra scrutiny, it could cause problems. We wanted his trip to be as problem-free as possible, so we would have to make special arrangements to get him through the airport and on his way.

The Transportation Security Agency did not exist at the time but the U.S. Immigration Service did, and it had an officer assigned to CTC whose job, among other things, was to provide assistance in situations like this. First thing on Monday morning, I met with the immigration officer to discuss how we could get Pasha through the airport without a delay and without causing undue concern among other passengers. Although for operational security reasons, I could not tell the officer what Pasha would be doing for us, he understood enough to know that it was important, and he was eager to help. With his assistance, arrangements were made for Pasha's travel.

On the night of his departure I picked him up at a predetermined location in northern Virginia. On the drive to Dulles Airport, I went over the contact plan for when Pasha would be met again in two weeks time. The meeting would take place in Pakistan's capital, Islamabad. I did not know for certain that I would be the officer to meet him, so I gave him a verbal parole that would be used in the event that he met with a different CIA officer.

At Dulles, Pasha and I met the CTC immigration officer and a couple of his colleagues at an auxiliary gate where I had been instructed to go. Pasha and I got out of the car and transferred his bags into an unmarked van. This would be the last time I would talk to Pasha in the U.S., and it was time to say good-bye.

"Alright, my brother, this is the first step. Either myself or one of my colleagues will see you in Islamabad. Remember what we talked about. You need to come to the meeting with a full report on what's going on back home. That will be what determines the next steps we take."

"No problem. I am ready to do this."

After a quick embrace, Pasha got into the van that headed off for the terminal building. One of the immigration officers escorted me to a room inside the terminal where we would be able to monitor Pasha's boarding of the aircraft via closed circuit television. I was beginning to get a bit concerned as most of the passengers had boarded and there was no sign of Pasha, when suddenly, seemingly out of nowhere, he appeared and got at the end of the line and boarded the plane. I stayed at the airport until his plane took off, and then returned home wondering if I would see Pasha again.

10

New Mission

Working WITH PASHA WAS mainstream case officer work, and it had been a nice diversion from the headquarters routine. But with his departure, I was back to sitting at a desk waiting for word on when I might deploy. It was now well into October, and a couple of other teams had deployed to northern Afghanistan. As they arrived in country, each team was usually assigned to work with a senior Northern Alliance commander. In addition to managing the CIA's relationship with the commander and collecting intelligence on events on the ground, the teams were also responsible for providing the Northern Alliance forces with material support, including weapons. The teams continued to be made up predominantly of paramilitary officers supported by a handful of medics with an occasional NE division officer with specialized area expertise thrown into the mix.

Also by this time, Special Forces teams began to deploy and join up with the CIA teams already on the ground. The ODA's brought with them a Special Operations Forces Laser Marker, or SOFLAM, that could be used to direct close air support for the Northern Alliance forces battling the Taliban and al-Qa'ida on the Shomali Plains north of Kabul.

About this same time, it began to look like I might deploy as well—not to Afghanistan, but to Pakistan. A foreign liaison service had approached the CIA saying they had a cross-border agent network that could provide reporting on the Taliban and al-Qa'ida, and they were offering to work jointly with the CIA on running the network. I was teamed up with a paramilitary officer for the mission, but before we got very far into the planning, the liaison service advised that there were some doubts about the credibility of the network, and the offer to cooperate was withdrawn.

With another deployment possibility gone, all I could do was hope that Pasha's efforts in northern Afghanistan would be successful. If they were, the tentative plan was for me to take in a team to link up with him. In the meantime, I was back in waiting mode.

During this time, most of the day to day routine was unremarkable. One day, however, President George W. Bush came to the Agency to give a talk to the employees. He offered encouragement and thanked everyone for their around-the-clock efforts since the 9/11 attacks. I didn't attend his speech, as there wasn't enough room for every employee to be there. But afterward, much to our astonishment, President Bush came down to the offices of CTC/SO, escorted by CTC Chief Cofer Black. We all dropped what we were doing and lined up in the bullpen area. The President, with Cofer beside him, walked along the line of employees shaking our hands. When they reached where I was standing, Cofer stopped the President and personally introduced him to me. President Bush thanked me for my work and the two then continued down the line.

I was stunned that Cofer had introduced me by name to the President of the United States. I had worked for Cofer in one capacity or another for the previous six years and had the highest respect for him. His gesture meant a lot to me.

Around the third week of October, I was called into the front office of CTC/SO, along with another NE Division officer named Jimmy. I really didn't know Jimmy well at that point, except by his excellent reputation. Before coming to the Agency, he had completed a full Army career retiring as a Command Sergeant Major from Delta Force. He then joined the Agency to work as a case officer. He was well known and well liked, and I immediately liked him too. In part this may have been because his personality and manner of speech reminded me so much of one of my favorite characters, "Gus," who was played by Robert Duval in the "Lonesome Dove" TV mini-series.

Upon arriving at the front office we were directed to see John, the Deputy Chief of CTC/SO. I had had a fair amount of contact with John since coming to CTC/SO and had developed a high respect for him due to the intense focus and direction he provided to the office. A former Navy officer, he had a trim build with a silver head of hair and a neatly trimmed mustache. Always well dressed, he reminded me of a middle-aged model in a men's clothing catalogue. John was also a devout Catholic, and he was the only CIA officer I ever heard speak of the soul in the context of operational work. On that occasion, which was not too long after the formation of CTC/SO, another operations officer and I were in his office discussing CTC/SO's mission.

"You men need to realize that what you will be involved in may well bear on the salvation of your very soul. You need to think about that. I'm talking about eternity and the things that you do in this life that can affect how you spend it. It is important that you are at peace with yourself and with God and with the actions you take."

I believe it was an honest and heartfelt commentary on his part. Faith was clearly an integral part of his life and something that he consciously factored into his thinking and decisions. I had no doubt he had already given much thought about the impact of his current work on the question of his own salvation. The fact that he was still on the job was evidence that he was at peace with the course he was taking. I felt the same way.

This time, however, when Jimmy and I arrived in his office, there was no talk of salvation. John did not mince his words or waste our time.

"Gentlemen, things are moving along in northern Afghanistan, but we've got nothing going in the South. The Taliban and AQ are still in control. We need you two to get out to Pakistan and work with Station to get things going in the South. Any questions?"

Jimmy and I looked at each other and then looked back at John. We shook our heads.

"Good. Get your visas and travel reservations lined up. We want you out there as soon as possible."

"Roger," Jimmy replied and we started for the door.

"One more thing."

We stopped.

"I don't expect to see you two back here anytime soon."

Jimmy and I glanced at each other, and as we walked out of the office Jimmy turned to me and said in his folksy, southern way of speaking, "I do believe that was the shortest 'frag' order I ever did receive."

Although John had not explicitly said it, his instruction to "get things going in the South," referred to one thing: the capture of Kandahar, the crown jewel of the Taliban movement, and what would probably become al-Qa'ida's last major sanctuary inside Afghanistan.

I don't recall what, if anything, I said to Jimmy, but I do remember that I was satisfied. At last I had a mission, and it was a good one.

11

Pakistan on My Mind

It TOOK US A few days to get our visas and make travel arrangements. Meanwhile we had to purchase the gear we might need. Except for armored vests, CTC/SO didn't have equipment to issue out, so instead officers were given an equipment and clothing list and provided a cash advance to make purchases. Finding all the items on the list in northern Virginia, particularly the clothes items, turned out to be a challenge. It seemed as if everyone in the U.S. government was out shopping for the same things. Trying to find a couple pair of heavy-duty cargo pants with a 34-inch waist or size 11 hiking boots proved almost impossible.

Although Jimmy and I were to focus on establishing operations in southern Afghanistan, because I was due to arrive in Pakistan soon, it looked like I might be in a position to meet with Pasha when he came out of Afghanistan. Discussions had continued at CTC/SO about possibly putting a CIA team in country to work with him. Since I was the officer who had re-recruited him and prepped him for his mission, I continued to be the logical choice to go in with him should the decision be made to do so. I had mixed feelings about this.

The idea of working with Pasha to try to detect al-Qa'ida moving into his home province in the rugged Hindu Kush would be a challenging and worthwhile endeavor, and on the practical side, the money I had spent on snow shoes and a sub-zero sleeping bag would not be wasted. But there was a stronger allure about the idea of working in southern Afghanistan. Unlike in the north where CIA had a still small but growing presence working with the Northern Alliance, operationally and tactically speaking, the South was a blank canvas waiting to be painted. There was no "Southern Alliance" that held territory or had an army with which we could join forces; the Taliban and al-Qa'ida were still in control there. Whatever we did in the South had to take into account those very different circumstances.

But those were challenges for the future. Before we could begin to tackle them, Jimmy and I first needed to get to Pakistan. Though I had previously served in the region, I had never been to Pakistan. I knew facts about the country and its government, but my personal experience related to Pakistan and its people was very limited. My closest experience and most memorable impression happened years earlier when I was in the Army. I was attending the Special Forces Officer Qualification course and had the opportunity to work with a Pakistani Army captain who was a member of my student team. He was in the course as part of a military services exchange program between the U.S. and Pakistan.

The captain was from a Pak commando regiment, and although the oldest soldier in the course, he consistently scored the highest physical fitness scores and always managed to be the first to finish our daunting obstacle course. From a physical fitness standpoint he was an animal, to be sure. However, his intellect and manners were also of the highest order, reminiscent of an Oxford-educated English gentleman, a comparison with which the captain's accent aligned as well.

The captain and I were paired up throughout much of the training, so I got to know him fairly well—and in one instance almost too well. That incident occurred during a nighttime parachute jump into a national forest in North Carolina, which was the start of the course's final exercise known as "Robin Sage." The drop zone was tiny—"postage stamp" size, to put it in airborne vernacular, and it was going to be a challenge to hit it and avoid going into the unwelcoming branches that stretched up to us from the surrounding trees. We had exited the aircraft one after the other, but as my parachute deployed with a reassuring jolt, I realized that the Pak captain and I were very close to one another—dangerously close. The captain saw this as well, and we quickly steered away from each other to avoid our parachutes becoming entangled and collapsing. Safely separated, we turned our attention to reaching the unlit drop zone. As we floated through the moonless night above the trees, we suddenly found ourselves again coming toward one another, this time on a direct collision course. Fortunately, we just managed to avoid direct impact, but our parachute canopies, like the skirts of twirling dancers, brushed against one another as we passed by. Despite the dangerous distractions of our aerial ballet, we both made it to the drop zone unharmed. All but one of our remaining team members crashed into the trees, however, with the sounds of breaking branches shattering the silence of the night.

The scenario for the Robin Sage exercise was that our 12-man Special Forces A-team was jumping in "behind the lines" to link up with a guerrilla, or "G", force. The team's mission was to act as a force multiplier by training and advising the guerilla force on how to fight and defeat the conventional military forces of an authoritarian regime. It was during Robin Sage that I got to know the captain the best. At one point, he and I were teamed together to conduct a two-day reconnaissance of a guarded bridge that served as the target of the exercise. To be successful—and not be discovered by the bridge guard force—required great stealth and patience, and there was almost no talking between us as we scouted the bridge's defenses during the days. However, at night we would quietly withdraw from the bridge and move deep into the woods to set up a primitive lean-to made of rain ponchos. We would roll out our sleeping bags under the shelter and try to get some rest. As we lay there listening to the sounds of the night, in a lowered voice the captain talked about his home and country. He was extremely proud of Pakistan and the Pakistani Army, telling tales of battles that had been fought in the many wars against India and the heroics performed by Pakistani soldiers. Despite the bloody history of conflict between India and Pakistan, the captain said he believed peace was possible one day, although it would be "a long time coming."

As I thought about Jimmy's and my upcoming trip to Pakistan, I remembered the captain and how impressed I was by him. I wondered how his Army career had turned out and what he thought of the current situation in Pakistan. His impression on me was so strong and lasting that some eight years later he would be the inspiration for the fictional character, Major Tarek Durrani, the protagonist in my novel *North From Calcutta*.

12

Saying Goodbye

Our FINAL PREPARATIONS FOR the trip to Pakistan included getting our shots updated and drawing body armor from CTC/SO. Between the body armor, sleeping bags, rucksacks, and clothing, to include cold weather gear, we had a lot of "stuff." To transport it, I purchased a black waterproofed North Face wheeled duffle bag and managed to get most of the gear inside. The remaining items I packed into a large REI rucksack.

The last couple of days before leaving were a blur as Jimmy and I made our final preparations for deployment. During that time, however, a few events stood out. One occurred when I was catching an elevator to the 6th floor at Headquarters. When the doors opened, there stood George Tenet alone in the elevator, his trademark cigar sticking out of his coat pocket. I liked Tenet as a director. I believed he was the best director that I had served under, beginning with Bill Casey who was the director when I joined CIA. I had only met Tenet a couple times, most recently during a COS conference a year earlier. I doubted he would remember me so I extended my hand and introduced myself. Shaking my hand and smiling, he asked where I was assigned. I told him CTC/SO and that I was headed out to Pakistan, hopefully en route to Afghanistan. As the elevator stopped at the 6th floor and I started to get off, a serious look crossed his face. Just before the doors closed he said, "Be careful out there. Don't take any chances that you don't have to."

Another memorable event during that time was what was probably the most serious conversation I have ever had with my wife. We were still living at the Oakwood apartments while we waited for our household goods to arrive from overseas. One evening after work, we were strolling through an old cemetery behind the apartments reading the gravestones, some with dates from the 1700's carved into them. I decided to tell her that I would be leaving very soon and I wanted her to understand why I had to do this. As I debated on how to bring it up, I realized that perhaps a cemetery was not the best venue for the conversation, and so I waited until we were walking down the sidewalk alongside a quiet residential street.

"It looks like I'll be leaving in a few days and I think this time it's for real. But I won't be going to Afghanistan, at least not right away."

She did not appear surprised. I had been trying to deploy for weeks, but I knew the word that I was finally leaving would hit her hard.

"Where are you going?"

"Pakistan."

"Do you know how long you'll be gone?"

"No. I suspect at least a few months."

There was a pause in the conversation as we continued to walk.

"I want you to know that I didn't volunteer for this because I'm trying to get a promotion or that I'm trying to be a hero. I'm doing this because I have to. This is what I'm meant to do. I've known that from the moment of the 9/11 attacks."

I had already come to terms with the possibility that I might not come back alive, although I didn't tell her this. I had participated in some potentially deadly activities in my life, but the risks in those instances were relatively low, well calculated, and well understood. This time, though, there were simply too many unknowns to be able to evaluate what all the risks would be. It was really the first time I felt at a deep level that what I would be doing could cost me my life, and cost my family a husband and father. It would be a terrible price to pay. But each time I had considered the risks, I also remembered the thousands of Americans who had been murdered at the hands of al-Qa'ida. I also thought of the victims' families and friends who had to endure the unimaginable pain of their loss. And was there any reason to believe it wouldn't happen again? I certainly did not seek or want to die, but I knew if there was any cause that was worth dying for, this was it. I also knew that there were plenty of Americans who would have done anything to trade places with me, and I recognized what an honor and privilege I had been given to serve my country at this critical moment in history.

My wife did not really know or understand the full scope of what my work would entail, but she certainly knew some risk was involved. Still, after 23 years of marriage, she also knew me better than anyone.

"I know you have to do this," she said, "And I understand why you're doing it. Just be safe and come back home to me as soon as you can."

"I will. I promise you I'll be back as soon as I can."

That conversation was my way of making peace with her. If I were killed she would know that at that moment in time, there was nothing more important to me and that I had believed in what I was doing with all my heart. I have no doubt, particularly in those early days with the horror of 9/11 still present in everyone's mind, that every member of the small group of Americans, both CIA and military, who found their way to Afghanistan went there with the exact same belief and feelings that I had.

PART TWO

PAKISTAN

13

Islamabad

Jimmy AND I DEPARTED for Dulles Airport directly from Headquarters in an Agency motor pool van late one October afternoon. The trees along the Dulles Access Road glowed in shades of gold and red as the sunlight washed through them, and I felt a tug of regret that this would likely be my last look—for this year at least—at the glorious crescendo of autumn color. Like the taste of a great wine, I tried to savor it for as long as I could.

At the airport I turned my attention to the reality of the trip at hand, and Jimmy and I began the routine for boarding an international flight. Not surprisingly, when we checked in at the counter our duffle bags and rucksacks were considerably over the weight allowance, and each of us paid close to a thousand dollars in excess baggage fees.

We boarded an overnight flight to Paris, arriving at Charles De Gaulle Airport in the early morning just after dawn. Our connecting flight to Islamabad did not leave until later that afternoon, and I wasn't looking forward to the long layover. As it turned out it wasn't so bad. Jimmy and I were unexpectedly directed to a small room inside the transit lounge. It had a couple of couches, and since we had the place to ourselves, we decided to stretch out and catch up on some sleep. We never knew why we were given this special treatment by the French. It may have had something to do with our unusual check-in luggage, which included holsters, two bullet-proof vests, GPS's, knives, and an assortment of outdoor gear. Whether the reason for the special treatment had to do with a desire to keep us isolated out of security concerns or not, we appreciated the privacy all the same.

Late that afternoon we boarded a British Air flight to Islamabad, arriving there after dark. A station representative expedited our processing through Pakistani Customs and Immigrations, and we went directly to a modest hotel in an out-of-the-way part of town. The next morning, very much jet-lagged, we reported to the station.

Our first stop was with the Deputy Chief of Station, or DCOS, whom I knew but had never worked with. The meeting did not go well. It quickly became apparent that Jimmy and I, as members of CTC/SO, represented the enemy in the DCOS's eyes. This was not completely unexpected. Anyone who had read the cable traffic between the station and CTC/SO over the previous weeks could pick up on the friction and tension that existed. Tension between Headquarters and a field station is not that unusual even in routine operational matters, and can even have some positive benefits, a check-and-balance system so to speak. But in this case, the CT effort we were engaged in was not routine. The situation was further exacerbated by the fact that up until the 9/11 attacks, because there was no CIA station in Afghanistan, the station in Pakistan served as the de facto station-in-exile for Afghanistan. That meant Islamabad station had taken primacy on all things Afghan. With the creation of CTC/SO, the station's role in relation to Afghanistan had changed from being the lead player to a supporter, albeit a critical one, given its regional location and its resident expertise on the country. To hear the DCOS talk, however, it was as if nothing had changed. He reacted as if CTC/SO was just another Headquarters element, and Jimmy and I were just two more TDY'ers sent out to support the station.

After listening to what Station wanted to do—or at least what the DCOS wanted to do—which varied significantly from what CTC/SO envisioned for the future, I sketched out CTC/SO's plan for the way ahead in southern Afghanistan. The central tenet of the plan being to put CIA teams on the ground in support of as-yet-to-be selected Pashtun tribal leaders willing to take on the Taliban and al-Qa'ida in their own backyard. This plan was not unknown to Station as it had been communicated and discussed in cable traffic at some length. Still, it conflicted with Station's approach. Its management believed that ongoing efforts to negotiate with key members of the Taliban government to give up al-Qa'ida members in Afghanistan could still bear fruit.

"Station calls the shots on Afghanistan, and we're not ready to endorse this strategy," was the essence of the DCOS's response.

"Even if you don't endorse it, you need to support it. CTC/SO is responsible for CIA's effort in Afghanistan, and it wants to move forward in the South as quickly as possible. Station's support is essential to this," was the essence of my rejoinder.

"No one told me SO is in charge," the DCOS said, a defiant look on his face.

I found it hard to believe that he really did not understand that SO was in charge of the Afghanistan initiative, but I took him at his word.

"Then I'm telling you. CTC/SO is responsible for directing all CIA activities in Afghanistan. Everyone recognizes the key role this station has to play in the effort but SO is in charge, not the station."

It was an uncomfortable moment and I thought it entirely possible that Jimmy and I would be on our way home the next day.

Fortunately, we weren't sent home, and a few days later, the COS called us into his office. Since our arrival, we had not seen much of him as he was a busy man, frequently in meetings, including meetings with the U.S. Ambassador, Pakistani President Musharraf, and the leadership of the Inter-Services Intelligence Directorate (ISI), Pakistan's premiere intelligence service. My face-to-face impression of the COS matched with what I had previously heard: he was a serious-minded, smart guy who knew his stuff. After seating ourselves, the COS looked up from the cable he was reading.

"Headquarters has decided to support Hamid Karzai with an agency team. You two, along with our officer, Greg, as the team leader, will form the advance element of Echo Team. We're making arrangements to get you down to a Pak airbase in Jacobabad ASAP to link up with the U.S. Air Force Special Ops Wing. They'll be supporting your infiltration into Afghanistan. A paramilitary team out of Washington will join you there in a few days and bring the gear and weapons you'll need."

The COS didn't need to explain who Hamid Karzai was. A respected anti-Taliban Pashtun leader, Karzai was now inside Afghanistan trying to foment a rebellion against the tyrannical regime.

After a few minutes of discussions, we departed the office. Once again, a short conversation was sending Jimmy and I closer to our intended destination.

I had not met Greg, a career paramilitary officer serving on assignment in Pakistan. Based on his reputation, which some would say was legendary, I expected him to be physically big and extroverted. When I met him later that day, I saw that he was of medium height and build, hard-as-nails fit, and that he had a reserved personality and the respectful manners of a properly raised Southerner. His bushy oversized mustache seemed a throw-back to the Civil War, and was a contradiction to his otherwise unassuming nature. More important than my first impressions of Greg was Jimmy's high regard for him. Jimmy had known Greg for many years, going back to the time when Greg was a lieutenant in the Marines in Beirut. Jimmy's endorsement was all the bona fides I needed.

I still had unfinished business with Pasha, but because of our new orders, I would no longer be able to work with him, and a station officer took over the case. For reasons I never had the opportunity to learn, the plan to put a team in with him in northeastern Afghanistan never came to fruition. All the work and planning we had done with him in Washington came to naught.

Greg, Jimmy, and I left for Jacobabad the next day. The COS, DCOS, and a couple of others walked us out to the waiting van to say goodbye. I appreciated their taking the time to send us off, and even the DCOS seemed to have decided we weren't so bad after all. There was something subdued about their demeanor that caught my attention, however. And then I saw it in their eyes: they believed they might well be looking at dead men walking. It reminded me of when I had once said goodbye to a beloved elderly uncle. I remembered thinking as I looked at him that I would probably never see him alive again. There must be something telling about such a look, as I could see in my uncle's eyes that he knew exactly what I was thinking, just as I knew what the members of this send-off committee were thinking. My uncle had proved me wrong and lived long enough for me to see him again. I hoped we would all do the same.

The van drove us to the military section of the airport in Islamabad where a Pakistani plane was waiting. Onboard the plane our mood was somber. I don't think any of us spoke during the entire flight, each lost in our own thoughts about what we had left behind and what was to come.

14

Karzai

The PAK AIRCRAFT DROPPED us and our gear at the end of a desolate runway bathed in the warm light of the mid-afternoon sun. Without so much as a word from the crew, the plane immediately turned around and took off, disappearing into a cloudless sky.

An arid landscape surrounded us and there were no buildings nearby, but we spotted a pickup truck parked alongside the runway several hundred meters away. Greg jogged over to it and convinced the sleeping Pakistani occupants to give us a ride to an aircraft hangar we could see in the distance. The truck took us most of the way, but the driver wisely let us off before reaching the fenced security perimeter. We walked the rest of the way, and as we neared the first band of concertina wire, I noticed two machine gun positions that were dug into the barren ground, reinforced with sandbags that formed parapets. U.S. Marines, who eyed us warily as we approached, manned the guns. We had no official identification to present, and we told them we were from Islamabad and were looking for the Air Force Special Ops Squadron. Apparently convinced we were friendlies, they pointed out the way and let us pass through the entrance gate.

We found the squadron headquarters located in the aircraft hangar which had been divided into work and sleeping areas. The Air Force personnel were working in shifts so some people were asleep, or at least trying to sleep, though it was in the middle of the afternoon and fully light inside the hangar.

In Islamabad, we had been told to ask for Colonel Steve Hadley, the air operations commander. We found him asleep on a cot, and an airman rousted him from his slumber. He looked exhausted but that didn't stop him from immediately getting up and tending to our needs. In the coming days I would learn what an impressive guy he was. Not only was the colonel a helicopter pilot, he was also a medical doctor and, like myself, an Army Ranger School graduate. He had an eclectic range of talents, to say the least. Quick with a smile and always in an upbeat mood, he was very personable. I think all three of us liked him immediately.

Colonel Hadley was one of only a handful of Air Force personnel who were briefed on who we were and the nature of our mission. Others who were briefed included members of the intelligence staff, one of whom was a young Air Force Captain named John Smith. Because of the restricted number of briefed personnel, Colonel Hadley and Captain Smith would be our principal contacts during our time at the airbase. Over the next couple of weeks they were an incredible support to us in our preparations for infiltrating Afghanistan. Colonel Hadley's support would prove to be even more impressive and critical in the days following Echo team's insertion into the heart of Taliban territory.

We had only been in Jacobabad a couple of days when we received orders to pull Karzai and his tribal elders out of Afghanistan ASAP and to bring them back to Jacobabad. Karzai and his fledgling anti-Taliban insurgency's tactical situation had deteriorated to the point where they were on the verge of being cornered and annihilated by the Taliban. Using a CIA communication link with Karzai that had previously been established, arrangements for how his rescue would be accomplished were worked out. The plan called for Greg and Jimmy along with a small SEAL team to carry out a helicopter extraction. I was disappointed that I was not going to be part of the mission, and I approached Greg about being included. But he refused my request, saying he didn't want to risk any more people than necessary.

I couldn't argue with his logic about risking additional lives, so I suggested that I take Jimmy's place. Jimmy had participated in just about every U.S. military undertaking since the Vietnam War, and he had twice been in helicopter crashes, one of those during a combat mission. I felt he had done more than his fair share of risk-taking for his country, particularly when compared to the comparatively minor risks I had taken.

"This is the real deal," Greg responded. "If something goes wrong, I have to have a clear conscience about the decisions I made for this mission, including who I picked to go. Jimmy has more extensive and more recent military experience than you do. I appreciate your willingness to go, but he is the best choice."

He was of course right about Jimmy. There was no way I could compete with his military experience—a full Army career, most of it spent with Delta. On top of that, Greg and Jimmy were close, having known each other for many years. I knew that counted for a lot as well. I, on the other hand, was an unknown quantity in Greg's eyes. While I was Army Ranger and Special Forces qualified, I had spent only six years in the military and had not worn the uniform in almost 18. There really was no argument to be made about which one of us made more sense to take on the mission, and I had to accept the logic of Greg's decision. So when the team departed to extract Karzai and his tribal elders, my role was relegated to staying behind to keep the home fires burning.

While the team was away, I went over to the hangar and talked to Captain Smith about getting some folding cots for our expected guests. He and I loaded them onto a pickup truck, brought them to our building, and set them up in the largest room available. I was not even sure the Afghans would want to use the cots, but I figured it would be rude not to make them available. If they didn't like the cots, they could always sleep on the floor.

Late that night, we got word that the extraction was successful, and the team and Afghans were returning to base. The extraction had been carried out using a helicopter, but once in Pakistani territory, all the passengers were transferred to an MC-130 fixed wing aircraft and flown to the airbase.

Captain Smith and I walked over to the motor pool and found a bus with the keys still in it that we could use to transport the passengers. It was an interesting drive over to the airfield, as neither of us had ever driven a bus, and we had to do it in the dark without headlights due to tactical restrictions. Fortunately we managed to get there without running anyone over.

The incoming aircraft was totally blacked out so in the nighttime sky we couldn't see the plane's approach. But we heard it land and taxi over to our location. Even when the plane was only feet away, it was almost impossible to see it without the aid of night vision goggles. Although the aircraft was now in relatively friendly territory, the SEAL team members were taking no chances. When the tail ramp came down, they were the first ones off, holding their weapons at the ready. They did not move quickly, however, and in the dim light that emanated from the interior of the plane, I could see the odd fashion in which they high-stepped down the ramp in order to minimize the chance of stumbling over the raised framework of the ramp floor. Only after they determined to their satisfaction that the area was secure did they permit the Afghans to file off the plane. The SEALS then loaded back onto the MC-130, which taxied away into the darkness.

I saw Karzai for the first time as he stepped past me to board the bus. Dressed in traditional Pashtun garb, his hands clasped and pressed against his chest, he nodded to me and in a voice not much above a whisper said, "Hello." His image and demeanor struck me as that of a religious figure, gentle and kind, hardly someone you would expect to have just started an armed rebellion against the Taliban regime.

15

A Full Up Team

W ithin A COUPLE OF days of Karzai's extraction, three paramilitary officers, Don, Will, and Ron, as well as Dave, a CIA Office of Medical Services physician assistant, arrived from Washington. At this point, Echo Team came fully into existence. Greg and Jimmy knew most, if not all, of the new team members. I knew none of them. They were a tight group, and I assumed that since I was not a paramilitary officer, it would take a while to gain their acceptance. The truth was, despite my own background as a former Green Beret and Ranger, I felt a little insecure about not being a member of their elite group. But that didn't last long, as I very quickly came to feel like part of the team.

Shortly after the paramilitary team arrived, we were all issued weapons and other equipment. Ron, a former Force Recon Marine who hailed from New York, was the team armorer and he handed out the weaponry. I signed for an AK-47 and a Glock 19. The AK was a new lightweight model made out of a type of wood I had never seen used before. Despite its light weight, I didn't like it. I was not used to the kind of fixed vertical fore grip carved into the stock, and the rear stock didn't fold. For practical reasons, like climbing in and out of vehicles and living in confined spaces, I wanted a rifle that could be made smaller when needed, and a solid stock wouldn't give me that option. I decided that once I was inside Afghanistan, at my first opportunity I would trade it for another one. I didn't tell Ron about my plan, however, as he seemed pretty proprietary about his weapons.

In addition to the AK's, we were issued magazines for them. Unfortunately, the team hadn't brought an extra tactical vest for me, so I had no way to carry the magazines other than stuffing them into my cargo pants pockets. Eventually I met an Air Force Sergeant who said he could lay his hands on a flight vest if I was willing to part company with the black Spyderco folding knife I wore on my belt. I had another knife so the deal was a no-brainer, and both of us walked away happy. The flight vest really wasn't designed for the purpose I had in mind, but it worked well enough. It also drew attention from the other team members; one said he thought it looked "sporty" and he even offered to trade his tactical vest for it. Realizing that my mates were envious of my warzone chic, vanity got the best of me and I decided that I liked the vest and hung onto it.

Other gear was issued as well, to include communications equipment, both radio frequency and satellite based, and Iridium phones. The robust commo suite would allow us to communicate with just about anybody we wanted—from aircraft providing close air support to wives talking about kids running fevers back home. For record traffic, there was also a team commo system used to communicate with CIA Headquarters and stations and bases around the world.

Soon after the arrival of the PM'ers, Special Forces Operational Detachment-Alpha 574, consisting of 10 men from 5th Special Forces group, joined us in Jacobabad. Normally, an ODA has 12 men, but the ODA was short one soldier and the team sergeant was delayed and would join us at a later date. The ODA's main role would be to call in air strikes in support of Karzai's forces. Additionally, they would advise the Afghans on tactics to use against the Taliban and al-Qa'ida. Special Forces ODA's were also capable of providing training to indigenous forces, but because Echo team and the ODA would be joining with Karzai's fighters already engaged in combat, deep inside enemy-held territory, there would be little time for training.

With the ODA's arrival, all the players were now in place to move the plan forward, and Karzai was anxious to get back with his fighters in Afghanistan. He was worried that his absence and that of his tribal elders would undermine the morale of his supporters and lead to their abandoning the fight against the Taliban. This was a concern that we all shared. We also recognized that Karzai's return to Afghanistan with Americans in tow would demonstrate America's commitment to their cause, and the sooner we could make that happen the better.

Planning sessions began immediately, and over the course of a few days a campaign plan was developed. It called for a helicopter insertion into the area of Tarin Kowt in Uruzgan province located in south-central Afghanistan, just north of Kandahar province. Tarin Kowt was chosen because it was where Karzai came from and he had many supporters there. The hope was that those supporters would swell the ranks of Karzai's fighters. Once a capable force was raised and equipped, the campaign to capture Kandahar would begin.

Kandahar was ground zero for the Taliban. It was the birthplace of the movement, as well as the political center of gravity for the Afghan Pashtuns. From a Taliban psychological perspective, when that city fell, even more so than Kabul, it would signal the end of any hope that they could continue as the ruling power in Afghanistan.

Aware of the importance of this effort, I found it extraordinary that the decisions on how to achieve this goal were being made by this small group of Americans working in concert with Karzai, and without interference from Washington.

During those days of planning at Jacobabad, I got to know the members of the ODA, some more than others. The two I spent the most time with were the team leader, a captain named Jason Amerine, and "Mag," the team Intel Sergeant. Interestingly, Jason at some point mentioned to me that he had applied and been accepted for employment with the CIA, but because the Army had instituted a "stop loss" policy after 9/11 he could not leave to take the job. If he was upset about that, I could not tell. Mag was a big, tough-looking guy. He had only recently taken on the role of the intelligence specialist on the team. He wanted to do a good job for the team, and he was interested in learning everything he could about intelligence. Aside from my time in Special Forces, my basic Army branch had been Military Intelligence, so I felt a connection with Mag and tried to serve as a mentor of sorts.

Sometimes, in the early morning, Mag and I would take our exercise together jogging around the airbase. As we ran along the sun-baked roads we would talk about the upcoming mission. Although he looked forward to it, his eagerness was tempered by a realistic and mature outlook about the dangers he and the team would face, an attitude I thought appropriate for someone serving in the role of the team's intel sergeant.

Another critical partner in our planning for the infiltration was the Air Force 20th Special Operations Squadron that would have the mission of inserting the combined CIA-Special Forces team into Afghanistan. The Squadron had ample capability and expertise for this kind of operation. Of particular importance from a planning perspective was the squadron's all-source intelligence section which brought to bear an impressive array of capabilities to include near real-time imagery, weather data, battlefield and threat analysis, and customized map products—all of which were used in the planning.

The intelligence section also was responsible for providing the pre-infiltration briefing to Echo Team and the ODA. The "enemy threat" portion of this briefing was particularly sobering. Up until the time of the briefing we had been focused on what we needed to do to get ready to deploy, and we had not focused heavily on what awaited us, although we certainly had a general idea. The threat briefing not only reminded us we were headed straight into "Indian country," it also provided details on the lethal capabilities the enemy possessed. By this time, Taliban and al-Qa'ida forces were largely being routed in the north, but in the South the situation was much different. With the exception of Karzai's fledgling armed-efforts and a couple of quick raids by U.S. special operations elements, no ground combat had taken place. Well-armed enemy forces numbering in the thousands still operated there.

About the only good news to come out of the briefing was that the area where we were going was not believed to have land mines left over from the days of the Soviet occupation, unlike some areas of Afghanistan which were saturated with them. Two things that I had always had an elevated fear of were snakes and lightning, both of which were hidden threats that could seemingly come out of nowhere and snuff you out. Putting those fears in a military context, land mines equaled snakes and artillery equaled lightning. So when the briefer said there were no land mines, this translated to me as "no snakes." That just left the lightning.

16

A Devoted Man

Although GREG, AS THE team leader, was in effect Karzai's counterpart, he had his hands full overseeing the infiltration planning, so he designated me to be Karzai's "go to" guy.

I occupied a room next door to Karzai and he took full advantage of my proximity, often calling out in his clear voice: "Duane, come quick. I have something very interesting to tell you."

This usually happened immediately after he finished a phone conversation with a political figure who had pledged his support to Karzai or had somehow otherwise encouraged him in his anti-Taliban campaign. When making these calls, Karzai by necessity, and despite international press reports to the contrary, had to maintain the fiction that he was still in Afghanistan fighting the Taliban. To do otherwise, would jeopardize the basis of his appeal for support.

It was through watching him and listening to his telephone solicitations, many of which were in English, that I began to realize the depth of his devotion to ending the Taliban's rule in Afghanistan, as well as its protection of al-Qa'ida. The man was tireless. Every waking moment of the day, every action that Karzai took, every word he spoke centered on one thing—ridding Afghanistan of the Taliban government. His single-mindedness was far beyond anything I had ever witnessed, and at some moment it hit me that I was in the presence of a man who was destined to become a historical figure.

At a personal level, I came to like him a great deal. It was hard not to. His cultured, genteel, and modest manner, reinforced by the crisp "Queen's English" that he spoke, combined to create an appealing personality. Despite the increasingly obvious fact that his importance and international stature were growing, never during the time I spent with him did he display any behavior that suggested a sense of self-importance—quite the opposite, in fact.

One evening, over a dinner of MRE's, the military's version of a "happy meal," the topic of the dangers ahead came up, prompting me to remind Karzai of the rather obvious point that given the support that was behind him, it was important that he didn't get himself killed.

"My life is unimportant. It doesn't matter if I live or die," was his response. "The only thing that matters is that Afghanistan becomes free of the Taliban."

One only had to hear the steel in his voice to know the statement was not bravado, but core conviction. I believed him, and why not? Karzai had already risked his life once by going into Afghanistan on a one-man mission to start a rebellion against the Taliban, and he was preparing to do it again. Only this time, he would not be going alone.

17

Off Again, On Again

After CLOSE TO TWO weeks since we had arrived in Jacobabad, we had a completed plan for the insertion. A date was set and pre-mission tensions began to mount. Then that date was cancelled and another launch date was set, and then that date was cancelled as well. The emotional roller coaster of the on again, off again launch date took a toll, at least on me, and I suspected it did on the others as well.

When another date was proposed, Greg was called up to Islamabad for a meeting to discuss the plan. This hadn't happened before and we took it as a sign that this time might be it.

When Greg returned he called us together.

"It's a go. We leave in three days when the nighttime illumination will be at its lowest."

I was elated by the news, but because I was not a paramilitary officer, I still had suspicions that, if push came to shove I might be cut from the team when it deployed. I was constantly trying to read the tea leaves about my status. Things seemed to be good, however, and I viewed my appointment as Karzai's go-to guy as a positive sign that Greg had confidence in me. There was nothing I could think of that suggested otherwise, with one possible exception.

There had been a couple of interesting things I had noticed about Greg during the time we had spent together in Jacobabad. One was that he rarely seemed to eat, and when he did, he usually was on his feet and in motion while doing so. That eating habit certainly helped explain why he didn't have an ounce of fat on his body. The other thing I had observed was that he did not have any socks; at least I never saw him with any on. I thought maybe when he had packed he had forgotten them so I offered him a couple extra pairs of mine, but he said "No," staunchly refusing to take them. I thought that was odd. The socks were clean; in fact, they were brand new and I had to wonder, why wouldn't he take my socks? But Greg was a hard guy to read. He never gave much away about what he was thinking, so I told the "sock story" to Jimmy to get his opinion.

"Don't take it personal. Greg doesn't like to take nothing from nobody. He would rather freeze his toes off. I'm sure he'll get some socks for himself soon enough—or maybe he won't. Either way, don't worry about him. He can take care of himself."

Since Jimmy knew him well, I accepted his explanation. But I still wanted to confirm I was good to go for the mission and decided to cut to the chase. I asked Greg if I was going in with the rest of the team.

"You bet you're going. Better start packing your shit," he said.

That was music to my ears. I had been working to get to Afghanistan since September 11th. I had missed my chance with Gary Schroen's team, and a couple of other opportunities as well, but finally it looked like I was almost there.

The next morning I walked over to the Air Force mess tent for a hot breakfast. The guys who worked there didn't know we were CIA and assumed we were aircraft maintenance contractors. I got a cup of coffee and helped myself to some bacon and eggs. I saw there was a news program playing on the big screen TV located in the middle of the cavernous tent, and I sat down at a nearby table to watch while I ate. A press interview with Secretary of Defense Donald Rumsfeld was on. Not surprisingly, Rumsfeld was taking questions about Afghanistan. In one of his comments he said that the U.S. had pulled Hamid Karzai out of Afghanistan and taken him to Pakistan. Rumsfeld went on to say that the U.S. was preparing to take him back in.

I was floored. The fact that we had taken Karzai out of Afghanistan was highly sensitive information, as was the fact that we were going to take him back. No one was supposed to know about it. Karzai himself had always denied he was outside of Afghanistan in his telephone calls to his supporters and international contacts, including the press. Now, a senior representative of the U.S. government had revealed the truth of the matter.

Not happy about what I had heard, I walked back to our building and relayed the story to Greg and the team. The first question on everyone's mind was whether we would still go forward with the plan as scheduled. Certainly from an operational security standpoint, Rumsfeld's statement was damaging, as Taliban and al-Qa'ida would know our intention was to bring Karzai back. With the element of surprise lost, their forces would be ready and watching. But they did not know exactly when or where his return would take place. It was kind of like the situation with Jesus or the 12th Imam: You've been told they are coming back, but the when or where of it was still unclear.

After due consideration by all involved parties, including CIA Headquarters and the military, the decision was that the mission would go forward as planned. Despite the increased risk, I think everyone was happy because we were more than anxious to get going.

18

New Team, New Mission

On THE DAY OF Echo team's departure, the nagging feeling that I would not be leaving with the team became a reality. The reason had nothing to do with my rejected socks, but with insufficient helicopter lift capability. So like extra baggage, I was scratched from the flight manifest and once again left behind.

After the team departed I, along with two SF soldiers who were also left behind, assumed a pessimistic attitude, believing there probably would not be a resupply flight anytime soon, leaving us stuck in Jacobabad. The next day, however, I received a secure-line call that changed everything: Headquarters wanted me to lead another team, designated "Foxtrot," into southern Afghanistan.

I was surprised by the call, and after I hung up it dawned on me that I would definitely not be joining back up with Echo team and Karzai. I was not sure how I felt about that. For the previous two weeks my every waking moment had been spent in preparation to go into Afghanistan as an Echo team member. I particularly didn't like the idea of parting ways with Jimmy, who had been with me from the start and whose extensive military experience and council I valued. Now it seemed Echo team was no longer in the cards. It was an abrupt change of course that I had to get my mind around.

The plan called for Foxtrot to infiltrate directly into Kandahar province and to link up with Gul Agha Shirzai, the former Kandahar provincial governor who had been driven from office when the Taliban had seized power. Like Karzai, he had recently begun building a force of mostly Pashtun anti-Taliban fighters inside Afghanistan. While I was intrigued by the operational concept, I had to admit that the idea of infiltrating directly into Kandahar province was a bit intimidating.

The next day, the U.S. Air Attaché in Islamabad and another Air Force officer flew down in a small plane to pick me up and take me back for discussions in Islamabad. Not knowing what the future would hold, I decided to bring all my gear with me, including my Glock and AK-47, which I just managed to fit into my duffle bag.

We waited until dusk to take off, and as soon as the wheels were off the ground, the Air Attaché immediately pulled the nose up putting the plane into a steep climb and then sharply banked to the left. The evasive maneuvers were not without justification. In the previous couple of weeks, some of the Air Force's planes had taken fire from locals who did not like the U.S. presence on the base, and one crewmember had been wounded.

I was impressed by the Attaché's flying skills, but began to have doubts about his navigation ability. Our route took us near the heavily militarized Pakistan-India border, and it was important that we did not stray into Indian airspace lest the Indians mistake us for a Pakistani plane and blow us out of the sky. Not long into our flight, the Air Attaché became uncertain as to our location in relation to the sensitive border. He was navigating by looking at landmarks, mostly lights on the ground delineating roads and towns, but decided that maybe it was time to consult a map. By this time it was dark and we were flying in black-out conditions so no interior lights were on. After digging through his bag, he found a red filtered flashlight to read the map, but the batteries were dead. Eventually, after dumping out the assorted contents of a briefcase, the pilots located new batteries, consulted the map, and got us back on course. All this sorting out seemed to take forever. Throughout the entire episode, however, neither of the Air Force officers was particularly ruffled, and we made it to Islamabad without any encounters with Indian surface-to-air missiles.

19

A Question of Leadership

The NEXT DAY I went into the station with my gun-concealing North Face duffle bag in tow to discuss the Shirzai initiative. Shirzai was not an unknown quantity. Even before I left Headquarters he was under consideration as a possible partner for the Agency to team up with inside Afghanistan. His deceased father had proven to be a fearless Mujahidin fighter in the war against the Soviets, earning the moniker "Shirzai" which translates into "the lion" of Kandahar. Gul Agha had also fought against the Russians and adopted his father's moniker, but he did not have the same reputation. His detractors believed any steel in his spine had disappeared during his years living comfortably in exile in Pakistan. As a result they had given him and his followers a less flattering moniker—"the Gucci Muj."

Because of these doubts, the burden of proof was put on Shirzai's back. He was told that if he could raise a sizable force of fighters inside Afghanistan, and if he demonstrated the capability to undertake offensive operations against the Taliban and al-Qa'ida, he would receive full Agency assistance, to include possibly having an American team co-located with his force. The fact that I was in Islamabad to discuss the plan to send a CIA team in to join him indicated that Headquarters, specifically CTC/SO, believed Shirzai had met the challenge and was ready for a team. It also meant that 20 years after participating in the Special Forces Robin Sage exercise I was about to actually do what the training had prepared me to do.

At the station, I had the opportunity to read the Headquarters cable that outlined the plan for Foxtrot team. I learned that CTC/SO wanted Foxtrot inside Afghanistan in four days, an ambitious timeline to be sure. I met with the Deputy Chief of Station to discuss how best to accomplish the plan. To my surprise, the DCOS, in a kindly, almost fatherly way, told me that despite what the Headquarters cable said, I would not lead Foxtrot team. Instead, Mark, an experienced Station officer who knew Shirzai, would.

I didn't really know Mark at the time other than to have talked with him for a few minutes when I was in Islamabad the first time through. He struck me as a good officer and someone with whom I'd enjoy working. But that wasn't the point. Headquarters had left no doubt in its cable that I was to lead the team, and while Station could challenge that decision, it had no authority to overrule it.

Of equal importance, putting Mark in charge didn't make sense. I outranked him and I had more years of operational experience than he did, including having served as a Chief of Station. I also had six years of military experience, including in Special Forces, with whom we would be closely working. Mark had zero military experience. While his knowing Shirzai was important and valuable, it simply did not trump all the other considerations regarding who was best qualified to fill the position of team leader.

I was in an awkward position. It was blatantly obvious that Station wanted its own officer to head the team, and I knew Foxtrot would have to rely heavily on the station for support, particularly in the preparation phase of the mission. I did not want to risk that support for the team by insisting that I be in charge. My goal was to get into Afghanistan, after all, not to be a team leader.

But there were principles involved here. I knew by any objective standard of measure I was better qualified to be the team leader, and Headquarters had designated me as such based on those qualifications. Short of Headquarters changing its mind, I decided I could not in good conscience accede to Station's wishes. Doing so would be tantamount to disobeying orders, and I so advised the DCOS.

The DCOS was not expecting pushback from me on the subject, and I could see tension and defiance come over his face as I tried my best to diplomatically enumerate the factors why it did not make sense for Mark to supersede me as team leader. My final point about the station having no authority to change the team leader since CTC/SO was in charge of the operation seemed to be particularly painful for him to hear. I did, however, tell him that if Station could persuade CTC/SO to designate Mark as the team leader then I would of course abide by Headquarters' decision and assume whatever role I was given.

While the DCOS excused himself to meet with the Chief of Station, I decided to go find Mark, as one way or another we would likely be working with each other, and we did not have much time left in Islamabad. In fact, a plane would be taking us to the airbase in Jacobabad later that afternoon. I asked someone where I could find him, and was told he was out of the office but was expected back at any minute.

"He knows he is joining Foxtrot and we are going down to Jacobabad later today, right?" I asked.

"No, I don't think so," an officer in the front office told me. "If you see him you might want to let him know."

That was a hell of a note. In just a few hours we were supposed to be catching a C-130 back to Jacobabad, and Mark hadn't even been told that he was going. When I found him I had to tell him the score.

If it was the first he had heard of the plan, Mark took the news well. He didn't throw rocks at me anyway. I also told him for the moment it was not clear which of us would be the team leader.

"I don't want to be the team leader," he said.

"Well, your station wants you to be."

Mark just shook his head and calmly headed off to pack up some clothes. I could not imagine what must have been going through his mind. I had weeks to psych myself for going into a war zone, team leader-designate or not. Mark had only four days.

By the time Mark returned and joined me at the front office, the strained atmosphere that I had felt earlier in the DCOS' office was gone. Quite oddly, as if there had never been any issue to begin with, I was told that Station concurred in my leading team Foxtrot. I never knew if it was my arguments that changed Station's position or some other factor, but I was thankful the leadership question was quickly resolved.

20

By the Seat of Our Pants

Mark AND I HAD little time to prepare and faced some serious, possibly show-stopping challenges, the first being that Foxtrot had no communications gear. Without communications, the team could bring little to the table in terms of helping Shirzai or reporting intelligence to Headquarters. Fortunately, steps were already being taken to address this issue, as well as that of Foxtrot only having two members. A CIA paramilitary team similar in composition to Echo's was being assembled in Washington and would be sent out to join Mark and myself. The incoming team would have the commo gear and the technical skills to operate it, not to mention that they all were expert warriors, trained to carry out intelligence operations in a combat environment. The catch was, the paramilitary team would not be ready until sometime after the planned infiltration date, and it would have to join us in Afghanistan at a later time. From my standpoint, not having the team from the get-go was less than optimal, to put it mildly.

There was some good news, however. The Department of Defense had approved sending another "A" team—ODA 583 from 5th Special Forces— to join with Foxtrot, and it would be in Pakistan in time to accompany us on the initial insertion.

While I was very happy to hear this, it did not solve the communications problem. The ODA had its own gear for military commo, but it would not have the gear Foxtrot would need for CIA operational and intelligence reporting. Communications remained a problem needing to be addressed.

Then I learned there might be a solution to our commo problem. A two-man advance element from a U.S. military Special Operations task force was in Islamabad and had commo gear that was compatible with Agency crypto. This was great news. I decided to walk over and meet them to discuss the situation with the goal of getting my hands on their gear.

On the way to see them, I spotted three people walking along the sidewalk, two of whom I recognized as being former "Shelter Now" hostages of the Taliban, and who only a day or two earlier had been rescued by U.S. forces. I knew the Agency had worked hard on their behalf and had arguably played the key role in getting them out of harm's way.

As I passed them, I paused to say, "Welcome back," and to tell them I was glad to see they were safe and sound. They clearly were delighted to be where they were and out of danger, and they told me it was all thanks to God that they had been safely returned. I thought about that for a second but decided not to debate the point, and continued on my way.

After looking around for a bit, I finally found the two military Spec Ops operators, Gary and Mike. Gary came across as a slow talking, laid back country boy, but his rank of Command Sergeant Major told me the "laid back" aspect should be viewed with circumspection. Mike was a Sergeant First Class and looked like he could have been Al Pacino's double in the "Godfather." I liked them instantly but they said the only way Foxtrot could have the gear was if they went with it. Clearly they saw this as their ticket to Afghanistan. I could not fault them for that.

In my COS assignment in Latin America I had worked on a project for several months with a similar team from the same task force. From that experience, I knew these guys were professional soldiers through and through, and I would have loved to have them detailed to Foxtrot. The problem was that the approval for them to deploy into Afghanistan, a war zone, could not be granted locally. It would require Secretary of Defense Rumsfeld's signature. To get that level of approval out of the Pentagon within four days would be a challenge to say the least. I was not optimistic about the chances of success, particularly given DOD's track record of taking many weeks to get the approval for the first Special Forces team to join up with the NALT in northern Afghanistan. Despite the skepticism, Islamabad station immediately submitted the request up the channels.

In later discussions with Station's communications officer, I learned that even if Gary and Mike were able to join Foxtrot, because of some software differences with their commo gear, Foxtrot still would not be able to send, or receive, any CIA text or other data. We would be limited to secure voice communications with Headquarters. Considering that we were going to be in a warzone and working at a tactical level, secure voice communications to Headquarters probably would not be all that helpful. But it was better than nothing until the paramilitary team from Washington joined us and brought in the right gear.

To help augment our less than robust communications capability, Islamabad station issued Foxtrot a commercial email system that we could route through an INMARSAT antenna. This system would allow Foxtrot to send emails via satellite to the station, which could then relay the emails over secure staff channels to Headquarters. Unlike normal Agency communications, this backchannel system was not secure, but it did have PGP (Pretty Good Privacy) commercial encryption that, according to the commo officer, was actually fairly secure. I was skeptical that the Agency would authorize use of this type of system, but I was assured it was an approved system. The catch was that it could be used only for *unclassified* communications. I could not imagine that anything worth sending would be unclassified, but under the circumstances I thought, *OK, whatever.*

After talking to Gary and Mike I returned to the station, where Mark and I had to deal with another problem. Mark didn't have a weapon. Understandably, he wasn't thrilled about the idea of stepping off a helicopter in the middle of the night in Kandahar province without one. We were told all of Station's weapons had been issued, but then a pistol, a Browning 9mm High-power, was found in a safe drawer. There was only one magazine, however, and no holster or ammunition. Mark and I searched the supply room, literally climbing on top of cabinets to check out the upper-level shelves. Our search paid off and we found a box of 9mm ammo but still no holster or extra magazine. Luckily, I had brought a concealed carry pistol belt from the States just in case, and I gave it to Mark. Had we not found a pistol for him, I would have given him not only the pistol belt but my pistol as well. He still didn't have a rifle, but at least he would be armed with something beyond a hope and a prayer when we first arrived in Afghanistan. We figured we would be able to get him an AK-47 from Shirzai's fighters pretty quickly after that.

Late that afternoon Mark and I loaded onto an Air Force C-130 and flew down to Jacobabad. During the flight I thought about the abbreviated deployment timeline and all the equipment and personnel deficiencies that Foxtrot faced. It hit me that the decision to send in a CIA team to join Shirzai seemed almost an afterthought, something someone had forgotten about and then remembered at the last minute. Certainly, it was a shoestring operation by any standard, and we would be flying by the seat of our pants. I knew at that point that if it was going to make a contribution in Afghanistan, in spite of its many challenges, Foxtrot had to become—for lack of better words—"the little team that could."

In the final approach to the airbase my thoughts shifted to more immediate concerns as the pilot put the plane through some hard turns and quick changes in altitude. I had flown nap of the earth before on approaches to drop zones when I was in the 82nd Airborne Division, but the evasive maneuvers the pilot steered the plane through exceeded anything I had ever experienced. When I saw the Air Force loadmaster lose his cookies, I thought, *Yep, this is some serious flying.*

PART THREE

AFGHANISTAN

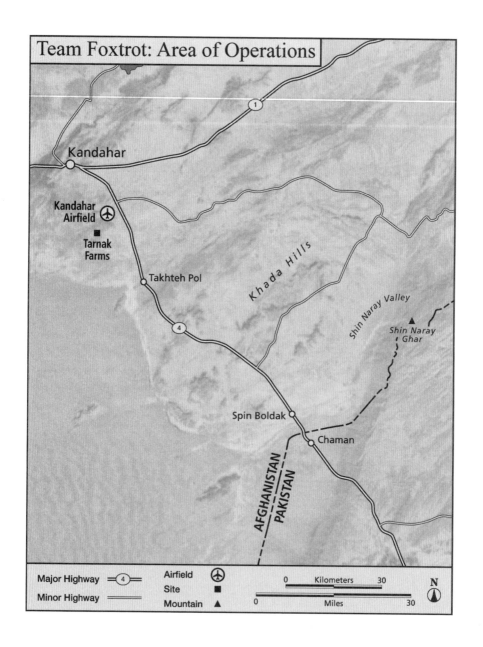

Team Foxtrot: Area of Operations

Kandahar

Kandahar
Airfield

Tarnak
Farms

Takhteh Pol

Khada Hills

Shin Naray Valley

Shin Naray
Ghar

Spin Boldak

Chaman

AFGHANISTAN
PAKISTAN

Major Highway
Minor Highway

Airfield
Site
Mountain ▲

Kilometers
0   30

Miles
0   30

N

Photo Gallery

1980. Ft. Bragg, NC. 313th MI Battalion, 82nd Airborne Division, following the promotion of battalion officers to 1st lieutenant. Author and his wife are the second couple from right.

The author (ca. 1980) on the "Green Ramp" about to board a C-130 for a parachute drop.

December 1981: Author (left) during "Robin Sage" exercise of the
Army Special Forces Officer's Qualification course.

Special Forces unit formation, 1982. The author is the first man in second file.

Top and bottom photos:
Members of Foxtrot, ODA 583, and Afghan fighters make preparations
for a road march from Shin Naray Valley base camp.

Author with Shin Naray Valley in background.

November 2001: Foxtrot team and ODA 583 preparing to depart base camp in Shin Naray Valley, Kandahar Province.

Shirzai's fighters observe US airstrikes in Kandahar Province near Takhteh-Pol.

The author just minutes after the capture of Takhteh-Pol village.

Shirzai's fighter raising the Afghan national flag immediately following the
capture of Takhteh-Pol from Taliban government forces.

November 2001: Inspection of captured Taliban tank by Afghan leader Gul Agha Shirzai, accompanied by a combat controller. The author is standing on the tank.

Foxtrot team's command post, Takhteh-Pol village.

Late November 2001: The author in the vicinity of Takhteh-Pol village, Kandahar Province.

Members of Foxtrot in defensive position at roadblock on Highway 4 east of Takhteh-Pol.

Author (left) with "Hank," the ODA 583 team leader, at the
Governor's Palace in Kandahar shortly after its occupation.

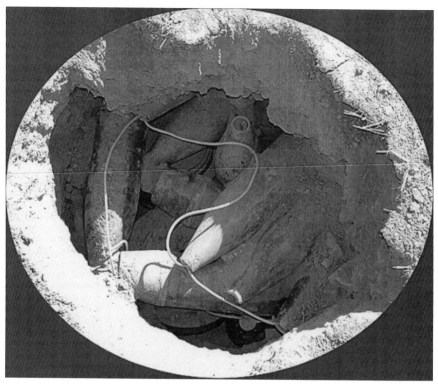

Rigged explosives discovered in the roof of the Governor's Palace in Kandahar.

Stacked explosives after being removed from the roof of the Governor's Palace.

21

There Be Snakes

U pon ARRIVAL IN JACOBABAD we moved into tents close to the airfield. Within a day or two, Special Forces ODA 583 came down from Karshi Khanabad, Uzbekistan, to join us. Other than brief introductions between myself and Hank, the ODA team leader, there was almost no interaction with the rest of the ODA for the first day or two. They kept to their area, and it seemed like they did not know what to make of us, or if they could trust us. I kind of understood that. We were the CIA after all, and God only knew what bullshit they had been told.

I decided that as it was entirely possible we all might die together in the next few days, it would be good if we got to know each other. So slowly we introduced ourselves to the ODA members and the ice began to break. Then we began in earnest our planning for the infiltration and link-up with Shirzai's fighters.

My experience from having been with Echo team during its pre-mission planning phase really began to pay off, as by now I understood what needed to be done and by whom. Just as I had seen with Echo, there were a myriad of details that had to be addressed. The next three days passed quickly and the date of our infiltration, 19 November, arrived.

I received word that the approval for Gary and Mike to deploy with us had just come in, and they would be arriving in Jacobabad soon. I was thrilled, having become almost certain the approval would not come through in time.

Islamabad was also sending down a paramilitary officer named Doug who had recently arrived from Washington. He would not be part of Foxtrot team but would stay in Jacobabad to set up a logistics support base for both the Foxtrot and Echo teams. He was also bringing down $500,000 for Foxtrot to take into Afghanistan.

When Gary, Mike, and Doug arrived, Doug immediately wanted me to count and sign for the money he was carrying. Mark and I were busy doing all the final coordination with the Air Force, Islamabad station, and Headquarters, and there was no time for us to deal with the money at that moment. We also did not have any place to securely store it, which meant someone had to be with it at all times. I told Doug his primary job for the day was to take care of the money and when I was free, I would sign for it.

I could tell Doug was not happy about that. He followed me around like a puppy dog, and several times during the day he asked me again to take the money. If I'd been him, I would have wanted to get rid of the responsibility for it as well. Despite my empathy for his situation, I finally got a little angry and came unglued on him.

"Doug, I told you. You've got one job to do today and that is to keep this money with you and do not lose it. When, and only when I tell you I'm ready for it, will you talk to me about it."

I knew he must have thought I was a jerk, but at least he didn't bother me anymore about the money.

Just hours before we were to board the helicopter for the air insertion, we received the enemy threat briefing from the squadron intelligence staff. It was the same drill I went through with Echo team, and it was a reminder that even though Kabul had fallen a few days before, there were a lot of bad guys still in the South. In fact, there were probably more than had been there before Kabul's fall. The briefers told us that the greater Kandahar area had an estimated 20,000 Taliban and al-Qa'ida fighters. An estimated 5,000 of these were believed to be in and around the city of Spin Boldak, which was near the Pakistani border. This was of immediate significance as our plan was to join up with Shirzai's fighters in the Shin Naray Valley north of Spin Boldak and then move southward to capture that city. After that, we would turn our sights to the primary objective of Kandahar, which was connected to Spin Boldak by Highway 4.

Highway 4 was of strategic importance in its own right as it was the only principal route to Pakistan from Kandahar. Al-Qa'ida frequently used the highway to move back and forth. By our controlling it, al-Qa'ida fighters would lose the use of the highway as a resupply and escape route.

While the number of enemy fighters was sobering, the final piece of bad news was almost as alarming. Unlike the area where Echo team had infiltrated, Foxtrot was headed to an area where there were heavy concentrations of land mines, i.e. "snakes."

22

Infiltration

After THE SECURITY BRIEFING I stopped by to thank Colonel Hadley, who had been invaluable in helping Foxtrot team over the last few days. With that accomplished, I finally had time to go to my tent to finish packing my rucksack. It was only minutes before we were to load on trucks and move down to the waiting MH-53 helicopter, and I told Doug I was ready for the money. There was no time to count it, however, and I just signed the receipt. Doug was all smiles. I did not have enough room in my rucksack for all of the money so I pitched Mark a couple of the cash bundles to stuff in his pack.

Mark had told me once that he knew he wanted to be a CIA case officer from the time he was a kid. Sitting in the tent, only minutes from our infiltration into Afghanistan, I wondered if he ever imagined he would be doing the kind of things he was doing now. At some point, I noticed Mark stopped his packing and just sat there on the cot, motionless. He was that way for a while, a distant look on his face, not moving, like his battery had just run out. I started to ask if he was okay, but I didn't. I didn't know what he was thinking, but I suspected the realization that we were about to go in was really sinking in. Finally, like a switch was turned back on, he resumed packing. I know I had had similar moments; probably everyone else on the team including the SF guys had, too.

As dusk fell we loaded our gear and ourselves onto a couple of pickups for transport to the helicopter. Contrary to our original plan, only a three-man advance element of the Special Forces ODA would be going in with us and not the whole team. Hank explained that the last minute change was mandated by 5th Special Forces Group Headquarters and was driven by SF doctrine that dictated that an ODA could not be infiltrated until there was confirmation that there was an indigenous force of at least 500 fighters present. The assumption was that a force this size could hold its own against any serious attacks. Once we had established that fact, the rest of the ODA would follow. The now reduced number of passengers meant that aside from the aircrew, there was only a total of seven men, consisting of Hank, his team sergeant, a third SF soldier, Mark, Gary, Mike, and myself. Our small number meant we only needed one bird. That was a good thing. With only one helicopter there would be less "brown-out" from dust blowing when we landed. This had been a serious and dangerous problem during Echo team's three-helicopter insertion five days earlier, which contributed to the team initially getting separated. Our helicopter would, however, be escorted by another bird that would not land except to rescue us in the event of an emergency. In addition, jet aircraft would be on station, ready to provide close air support for us if things went to hell at the landing zone.

Despite our small number, with the gear and the aircrew, the helicopter was tightly packed. I was glad it would be a relatively short ride, as the Shin Naray Valley was just a few kilometers across the Pak-Afghan border.

By the time we lifted off, it was dark outside. No lights were allowed on inside the aircraft so it was pitch black, and I discovered I had unwisely packed my night vision goggles in an inaccessible spot so I was effectively blind during the entire flight.

The helicopter flew with the rear ramp open with the tail gunner sitting in a rearward facing position. A few minutes into the flight he opened up with a burst of machine gun fire. The sound of the gun was unexpectedly quiet, but still, I was startled. It took me a minute or two to figure out that the gunner was just testing the gun. If they had said they were going to do that in the pre-flight briefing I had missed it.

Because of the lack of space, when we boarded I had to sit down on the floor with my rucksack still strapped on my back. It made for a comfortable backrest during the flight, but I knew that between the weight of the ruck and the crowded space, it was going to be a devil of a time trying to stand up and make a quick exit when we landed. After much thought, I decided my best hope was to use some netting that was attached to the inside wall of the aircraft. The only way I knew the netting was there was because I could feel it in the dark. When the crew chief gave the ten-minute warning, I grabbed the netting and began to pull myself up. It was a slow ascent. It was very hard to do in part because of the movement of the helicopter and also because we all were pressing against each other as we tried to stand. It took what seemed like several minutes and all my strength to grope and claw my way up the net into a standing position. There I was, on my "D-Day" assault into Afghanistan, and I was clawing and grabbing like a blind monkey in a cage. It was not how I had imagined it would be.

As we neared the coordinates of where the reception party should be waiting, the pilots were looking for three small fires set on a north-south axis. The fires were to serve as a reference marker to indicate where to land the helicopter. I knew when the pilots had seen the fires as I felt the helicopter start to slow and then begin a wobbly descent. For an instant we touched down, but then lifted back up, moved forward, then came back down harder than the first time, but not too bad, considering.

"Go, go," the crew chief yelled, and we started exiting out the rear of the aircraft. We were in two single file lines, one on the left side, one on the right. I was on the right side of the helicopter, and as I stepped off the ramp I was careful to avoid falling. Given the weight of my rucksack that was not easy, but I managed to alight safely. I immediately turned left to avoid the vertical tail rotor cutting through the air just a few feet away. Burdened by the rucksack, I stumbled away to get clear from the helicopter. Dust and sand driven by the prop wash made it impossible to see anything, even though I wore protective goggles.

After about 20 steps I ungracefully fell to the ground. As I fell, the rucksack slipped and its weight turned me sideways. I ended up on my back on top of the pack, like an upside down turtle. As I laid there in the most "non-tactical" of positions, the MH-53 lifted off into the night, its dark shape rising into the sky and moving away from me, taking the engine noise and prop blast with it. As it receded from view I managed to roll over. Silence descended, the dust settled, and I saw Afghanistan for the first time.

A sliver of moon hung low in the clear night sky, and I could barely make out the barren hills that overlooked the Shin Naray Valley. High above the valley, thousands of stars twinkled in the dark sky. The lovely nighttime scene reminded me of my boyhood home. *Hey, Toto, this isn't New Mexico*, I told myself.

I put the AK to my shoulder and assumed a defensive prone position. There was no gunfire, which I took as a good sign. I decided to try to stand up, and once again I had difficulty with the anchor on my back.

"You need some help?"

It was Mike, who had gotten off the helicopter just before I did. I stuck up my arm and he grabbed it and pulled me to my feet. After finding the rest of the group, we knelt down in the darkness alert for any signs of danger as we looked and listened for the reception party. At last we saw a blinking light shine in our direction. It was the recognition signal we were looking for, and we moved toward it. The light flashed a couple more times as we approached, and we soon saw the dark silhouettes of pickup trucks and men with guns. Then, out of the darkness an accented voice rang out, "Welcome to Afghanistan!"

Our greeter was an Afghan named Khalil who would become our number one go-to guy during our time in Afghanistan. He spoke English perfectly and was a cousin and right hand advisor to Shirzai.

We tossed our gear in the pickups, and along with other trucks filled with Afghan fighters providing security, we headed for Shirzai's base camp located a few kilometers further down the valley. Along the way Khalil told me that after the helicopter departed they couldn't tell that anyone had gotten out of it, and they were so disappointed thinking that at the last minute we had chickened out. Smiling a big smile through his beard he said, "Now that you guys are here with us, I know we are going to win!"

We arrived at the base camp, which was situated at a junction with a smaller valley. Next to where we parked, there was a small stream that had been damned up with rocks so that a clear pool of water a couple of feet deep and maybe 30 feet across had formed. It was the only surface water I would see during my entire time in southern Afghanistan.

We were led up a dusty trail to a dilapidated mud house on a hillside overlooking the water. As we walked we passed scattered groups of Afghan men squatting around small fires along the trail. Some looked at us warily. When we reached the house we saw that a green cargo parachute from a CIA supply drop made to Shirzai some days before was draped across it and served as the roof.

Inside there was a small room with an Afghan carpet on the floor. Lanterns and candles provided the lighting and a wonderful aroma of cooked food was in the air. The scene would have been romantic were it not for the AK-47'S laying all about and the several bearded men who sat around the carpet looking sternly at us as we entered. My first impression was that they looked a lot like the Taliban. My second impression was that they looked exactly like the Taliban.

One of them stood up and came over to us. It was Gul Agha Shirzai. He was a good-sized, barrel-chested man, in his late 40's, with dark hair, beard, and eyes. He was smiling broadly and gave each of us a welcome hug. As Khalil translated, Shirzai explained in Pashto how delighted he was that we were there. He told us he had a special dinner prepared in our honor and invited us to sit down and eat.

Before the meal was served, as we sat on the floor around the carpet, Shirzai made a little speech. He said he felt terrible about the 9/11 attacks and asked that we convey his condolences to the American people. He said he hated the fact that the people who were responsible were in his country, and he promised to help us find and get rid of them.

As Foxtrot's team leader, I felt obliged to reciprocate. Using Khalil as the translator, I told Shirzai and his lieutenants that we were happy to be there among such good friends, and together we would rid Afghanistan of the blight of terrorists. The Afghans nodded and made noises, best described as grunts, which I would later learn meant they agreed with what was being said. That was my initial firsthand lesson on Afghan culture and customs.

The food was brought out and we ate it communal style. If you wanted rice, you just reached in the bowl and grabbed a fist full. Custom dictated, based on sanitation concerns, that only right hands be used for this purpose. A poultry dish—chicken they said—was served. It was quite good, tender and very juicy. By the time we were done eating, our beards glistened in the flickering candlelight.

From the moment I had stepped off the helicopter, the night had had a surreal, otherworldly quality about it. At some point, I realized, it indeed was another world—it was Afghanistan.

23

Reflections on Leadership

The SPARTAN AND MILITARIZED life I would be leading in the coming weeks was a significant change from what my life had been before the 9/11 attacks. I was now in what the CIA would call a "paramilitary environment." The Army's designation for it was an "unconventional warfare environment." Whatever the description, it was certainly different than my former existence at Langley. Of course these kinds of surroundings were not new for me, but it had been a while. I was particularly grateful for my time in Special Forces, which had trained me specifically for the mission of working with a guerilla force behind enemy lines. But many years had passed since then so I knew that when it came to things military, I had to rely on the expertise of Gary and Mike, the two SpecOps task force personnel detailed to Foxtrot.

Still, not having current military skills did not absolve me of the responsibilities of being the team leader. Ultimately I was responsible to the Counterterrorist Center and the CIA for what we did or did not accomplish, as well as for the safety of Foxtrot's members. I took those responsibilities seriously even while I tried to maintain a light touch in my team leader role. Fortunately, in addition to having attended leadership courses at various times in my life, I could also draw upon some significant experiences from my time in both the Army and at CIA. Admittedly, none of those experiences had been in a combat environment.

My ideas about leadership and what the role entailed had been formed long before I came to Afghanistan. In fact, even before I joined the Army or the CIA. As a kid I was lucky to spend a lot of time with my father and, as I've alluded to before, his influence as a role model was significant. Most of our time together was spent outdoors, usually related to taking care of our livestock or hunting. Over the years I was able to observe him in many situations, and although I'm sure I didn't know it at the time, I was absorbing a lot of lessons that would shape my ideas about leadership and how to deal with people. When faced with a problem he was very deliberative in deciding on how he would solve it; he did not "shoot from the hip." He also was patient and slow to anger, and he never spoke badly of anyone or was disrespectful of even the poorest and most ignorant person. Completely unselfish, the needs of others always came first. But despite these positive traits, there was an underlying sternness about him, and my siblings and I were always on our best behavior around him, although he never raised a hand against us.

The fact that my father was in combat in World War II and Korea held a special fascination for me. Over the years I learned about some of his experiences, a couple of which surprised me, but gave me some indication of how he balanced the issue of mission and the welfare of the men in his charge. Two of the experiences occurred late in the Korean conflict when truce negotiations were ongoing and Chinese forces were pushing hard to gain as much territory as possible before an agreement was reached. Dad was a tank company commander with the rank of captain and his company was holding a defensive line that was constantly being hit by artillery and ground assaults. During a lull in the fighting a major with a film crew came up to the front from the battalion headquarters. Spent round casings, ammunition boxes, and ration cans littered the area. Apparently not pleased with the unsightliness of it all, and perhaps wanting a more pristine combat landscape to film, the major ordered my father to have his men get out of their tanks and police up the area. My father refused, telling the major that they were subject to being attacked and his men were staying in their tanks. The major became angry and threatened to bring insubordination charges against Dad. Suddenly an artillery barrage began during which the major happened to be wounded. Apparently, his wounds were not too serious, and to the dismay of the tank crews who witnessed the event, he was able to direct the film crew from his stretcher in filming his own medical evacuation from the battlefield. No charges were ever brought against my father.

During this same time period, Dad regularly received orders from battalion to send out nighttime foot patrols down into the enemy-occupied valley his tanks overlooked. The stated purpose for sending the patrols was to "keep up the aggressive fighting spirit of the men." Initially, patrols were sent out with the only result being men lost, killed, or wounded. Dad tried to get battalion to rescind the order for nightly patrols but the order stood. Finally, Dad just began to ignore the orders, and when queried about the results of the patrols he would advise there was nothing to report.

Upon hearing about my father's wartime actions when I was a boy, at first I was confused because I thought soldiers always obeyed orders no matter the consequences. But when telling me these stories Dad explained that sometimes leaders have to take care of their people even if it means not obeying an order, no matter the possible consequences for the leader. On the other hand, Dad told me of an experience where he took action when he had no orders, something else he said a leader had to sometimes do.

In that case a massive Chinese offensive was underway and a South Korean division had been smashed and was falling back in a disorganized, panicked route. Dad's company was ordered to move forward through the stream of fleeing South Korean forces to try and blunt the Chinese assault. As it happened, this attack had occurred on the same day that my father had turned over command of the tank company with orders to report to 8th Army headquarters to take over the security detail for General Maxwell Taylor. The new tank company commander who was to replace Dad was reported to have arrived at battalion but strangely could not be found. Dad technically was no longer in command of the company, but he knew the new commander, if he could be found, would be at a great disadvantage trying to take over in the middle of the Chinese assault. Dad knew the terrain, the tank platoon commanders, and the situation on the ground, so he decided not to leave for 8th Army headquarters. Instead he stayed with the company and continued to act as its commander. For the next three days, the Chinese assault continued during which Dad's company lost five tanks along with a number of killed and wounded. Dad suffered an injury himself when evacuating wounded from a knocked-out tank. The new company commander never showed up. Dad eventually was awarded the Bronze Star with a "V" device for his actions during the battle. Because he technically wasn't the company commander the award citation describes him as a "Special Advisor" to the tank company. I eventually was able to read official Army documents concerning this battle and the role my father and his company played in it. Years later Dad was told the destroyed hulks of his lost tanks had remained on the battlefield and served as part of the demarcation of the border agreed to in the Korean armistice.

Hearing these stories from my father had a huge impact on my thinking regarding the role of a leader. Even as a boy my takeaway was that taking care of and protecting your people was the most important thing you could do, because it was your people who were ultimately going to be the ones who would accomplish the mission.

*   *   *

My first formal introduction to leadership was through the Reserve Officer's Training Program (ROTC) at New Mexico State University in Las Cruces. The four years spent at NMSU were some of the most enjoyable of my life, and ROTC was perhaps the biggest reason why. ROTC became my fraternity, and through it I made friendships that last to this day. I also met professional soldiers who were assigned as the ROTC cadre responsible for our training. Almost all of the cadre were Vietnam veterans who, like my father, had had life and death experiences where leadership had mattered.

Undoubtedly the most influential of the ROTC cadre for me was Sergeant Major John Quirk, who had served in Vietnam as an Army Ranger and in the Korean War as well. A Boston native, SGM Quirk was the quintessential soldier and I got to know him well. In addition to his teaching responsibilities he was also the coach of the ROTC detachment's four-man orienteering team of which I was a member. A disciplinarian, he trained us hard in the use of a map and compass, and equally hard in our physical conditioning, running us for miles through the desert around "A" (Aggie) Mountain which overlooked the campus.

SGM Quirk used his involvement in the Orienteering program as a platform to continue the leadership lessons he sometimes taught from the lectern. Once during an overnight drive to an out-of-state competition, SGM Quirk told the team a story about an American infantry platoon that his unit had been sent to assist after it had come under nighttime Viet Cong attack. Unfortunately, by the time they reached the scene the battle was over and the platoon had been wiped out with 18 men killed. SGM Quirk said it was the worst thing he saw in Vietnam, and the memory of the faces of all those dead Americans soldiers was something he would never forget. The point he made was that it had happened all because the platoon leader had not insisted that his men dig foxholes after they had pulled into their patrol base for the night. Without the ability to get behind cover the men were easy prey for the VC, who had probably watched them move into the patrol base, waited until nightfall, and then attacked. It was a great failure of leadership about a simple thing, with disastrous consequences. It was stories like these, more so than the classroom theories on leadership, that really got my attention about the difference between a good leader and a bad one and the impact each can have.

SGM Quirk was transferred before I completed the ROTC program, but I saw him again on a mountainside in north Georgia during the summer of my junior year while I was attending Army Ranger School in lieu of the ROTC Advance Course. SGM Quirk was now the Command Sergeant Major of the mountain phase of Ranger School. We were in a patrol base when he appeared early one morning. He had come specifically to see me and a couple of my Ranger buddies also from New Mexico State. We all held him in the highest regard and felt honored by his visit, particularly knowing he had to hike up a mountain to get to us.

Ranger School itself is considered by the Army to be its most demanding leadership school. It utilizes small unit tactics such as patrols, raids, and ambushes as the leadership training vehicle. The training environment itself is arduous and requires the Ranger student to survive on two-thirds the normal food ration and an average of two or three hours of sleep per night for the duration of the eight-week course. Actually, our course was nine weeks because most of the students were ROTC cadets and an extra week was added to cover some additional subjects. Students are rotated into and out of leadership positions and evaluated on how well they perform. The evaluation process also includes a peer evaluation so there is nowhere to hide if you are not carrying your weight in the course. I was in the best physical condition of my life when I entered Ranger School and was a physical wreck by the time I finished it. Undoubtedly, it was the most demanding training I have ever endured, but it was effective, and to this day I believe I could still organize and lead a combat patrol.

Upon graduation from NMSU I received a 2nd Lieutenant's regular army commission in the Military Intelligence branch. After I completed the Basic Intelligence Officers Course I would be given the opportunity to put what I had learned and believed about leadership into practice. My first opportunity was as the Operations Security platoon leader in the 82nd Airborne Division. Much like what I would experience many years later in

Afghanistan, many of the men under my command were experienced professional soldiers. A quarter of the platoon was made up of non-commissioned officers, either Staff Sergeants or Sergeants First Class; another quarter was made up of Chief Warrant Officers, former non-coms who had become intelligence specialists. Many of the Sergeants and Warrants were Vietnam veterans. The other half of the platoon was lower enlisted personnel with very different specialties and work responsibilities than those of the experienced personnel. This situation created a real dichotomy in the make-up of the unit in terms of experience level and maturity. I knew my leadership style would require some flexibility, and the experience I gained leading this diverse group of soldiers was probably the best I could have hoped for. As a new 2nd Lieutenant, I constantly had to calibrate how best to address a particular soldier or situation, and I think I became a better officer for the experience.

I did make mistakes, however. In one instance I was designated to lead a detachment of about 10 soldiers drawn from across the MI battalion to support the 2/508th infantry battalion during its rotation through the Army's Jungle Warfare School in Panama. I met with the detachment soldiers to insure they knew all the operational and administrative details about our mission. The night when the soldiers were to report to me in front of their barracks, one of them, a PFC, arrived in a drunken state. Although from another platoon, I recognized him immediately. He had an unusually large head and because of the difficulty in fitting him with a standard helmet, he had been issued a test-bed version of a yet to be issued new helmet frequently referred to as the "Fritz" due to its similar look to the WWII-era German helmet. Given the size of his head and the distinctive helmet, he was hard to miss.

I was not happy that he had showed up drunk. In fact, I was pretty angry. I called the company First Sergeant who came down to the barracks. I told him I didn't plan to take the soldier with me when we went down to the infantry battalion, saying he would be an embarrassment to the MI battalion and he was in no condition to participate in an airborne operation. The First Sergeant talked to the soldier, who said he was sorry and begged to be allowed to go to the training in Panama. The First Sergeant and I stepped away to discuss the situation. He said the PFC was a good soldier, although he certainly had just screwed up. He also pointed out that it was going to be at least another 12 hours before we hit the silk over Panama and by then the soldier would be sober. The First Sergeant suggested I take the PFC down to the infantry battalion and talk to the company First Sergeant there and let him decide if he wanted him along. I was surprised that he was suggesting this course of action as I thought he probably would recommend disciplinary action be taken against the PFC. I liked and respected the First Sergeant, and while uncomfortable with the suggestion, I decided to follow his recommendation. Once down at the infantry battalion, which was assembling on a lighted football field, I laid out the situation to the First Sergeant there. He was a pretty rough looking soldier, with a haggard face and deep wrinkles in his forehead. A Combat Infantryman Badge and Master Parachutist Wings stitched onto his BDU's, he looked like he had seen a lot in career. He walked over to the PFC and looked him up and down.

"Where the fuck did you get that damn helmet, soldier?" he asked.

"They gave it to me because my head's too big for a regular helmet. The whole Army is going to get one in a couple of years," the PFC said.

"Jesus Christ, your head's too big?" The First Sergeant shook his head and chuckled. "Yeah I heard they're going make us all look like a bunch of Germans. Thank God I'll be gone by then. So you want to go to Panama, huh?"

"Yes, Sergeant."

"Once we get in that plane you going to throw up on my men?"

"No, Sergeant, I'll be okay.

"Alright, if you can show you can do a proper PLF (parachute landing fall) when we go through pre-jump you can go. But you better not fuck up down there. You're with the infantry now."

Listening to and watching the First Sergeant, I realized how the theory of leadership in the classroom is a far different thing than its application in the field. Similar to hitting golf balls on the driving range and then getting out on the actual course to play a game, there is a difference between the two, and only experience can bridge the gap. Had I left the PFC behind, yes, it would have been a form of punishment for his offense, but he would have missed an important training opportunity, my detachment would have been down one man, and the unit we were supporting would not have gotten everything they had asked for. By taking the longer view, the First Sergeant had made the right call, and the mission and everyone involved had benefited, including me. I had learned a good lesson.

After my stint as a platoon leader in the 82nd, I transferred to 7th Special Forces Group, also located on Ft. Bragg. I liked the SF attitude about leadership that came through in the Special Forces Officer Qualification

Course. The message was "be yourself." This was something my father had said as well. The basic idea being that if you don't have the personality and temperament of General Patton, don't try to be General Patton. You will be seen through immediately and you will not command the respect and loyalty that you will need to accomplish your mission. Throughout my professional career both in the Army and the CIA, I have seen leaders make this mistake, and it is quite striking how easy it is to recognize. It also is a mistake that is hard, maybe impossible, to recover from.

24

The Best Laid Plans

The PARACHUTE-SHROUDED MUD house in the Shin Naray Valley became our living quarters, and on the morning after our dinner with Shirzai I stepped outside to get my first daytime look at Afghanistan. From my elevated perch I saw that the wide valley we occupied was bordered on each side by steep, rugged hills sparsely covered by brown scrub brush. In any direction I turned, the land looked thirsty, and the air almost crackled from dryness when I breathed it. The arid character of the place made the pool of water below me look particularly inviting. The cumulative effect again reminded me of New Mexico, particularly southern areas of the state where as a boy I hunted desert quail, dove, and mule deer. The feel of the rifle in my hands, combined with the familiar-looking setting, put me at ease. I felt very much at home.

As our first order of business, Mark and I climbed into Shirzai's Land Cruiser, and he drove us around to show us his fighters so we could get a head count. They were not in formation, far from it, but were scattered in various small encampments up and down the valley, so the best we could do was to come up with an estimate. Hank was also taking a separate head count, and we compared notes at the end of the morning. I guesstimated there were 600–900 fighters; Hank figured the numbers were somewhat lower, somewhere between 500 and 700. Although our numbers differed, both estimates met or exceeded the magic number of 500. With that prerequisite met, Hank sent word back to 5th SF Group Headquarters and requested the rest of his team to be deployed that night as planned.

After we got back from the survey, I asked Shirzai for another AK-47, one with a folding stock and no vertical grip. A few minutes later a young Afghan wearing fatigues and oversized tennis shoes trotted up and handed me his folding stock AK. I did a functions check and the gun seemed fine. I handed him my AK and as he fondled the vertical grip I disliked, he smiled, probably because the gun was brand-new and considerably lighter than the one he had given me. To make sure the gun was reasonably accurate, I walked over to the backside of a hill and set up a dirt clod as a target. After pacing off a hundred meters I took aim and fired. The dirt clod shattered. The gun was good to go. In the meantime, Mark, who so far had only been armed with the Agency pistol, acquired an AK for himself.

Later in the day, Hank received word that the remainder of the SF team was not coming until the following evening. The original plan to have them come the day after we arrived had been scrubbed without our knowledge when the pilots who brought us in had reported to Air Ops that they spotted only about 40 fighters around the landing zone. Someone back in Jacobabad had erroneously assumed that they were the only fighters Shirzai had, so did not want to risk sending the rest of the team. Had they checked with us, we would have explained that the reason there were only a small number of fighters at the LZ was that we had instructed Shirzai to keep the numbers down; we did not want a lot of people present when we landed, which could've made it harder to identify friend from foe if something went wrong.

Around the time we learned that the remainder of the ODA was delayed, Khalil told us that the night we arrived, the local Taliban commander and a couple of his sub-commanders were present at the base camp talking to Shirzai about the possible surrender of the Taliban garrison located at the mouth of the Shin Naray Valley, only a few kilometers away. No deal had been struck, but the Taliban commander had requested a second meeting that had been set for that very night.

Khalil confirmed that we unknowingly had walked right past the Taliban delegation when we had first climbed the hill to the mud house. No doubt, that was the group that had cast wary glances at us as we tromped by. This meant the Taliban now knew there were Americans on the ground with Shirzai, a fact we had hoped to keep secret for as long as possible. To our chagrin, we now knew that the secret had only lasted for about an hour after we arrived in country.

We met with Shirzai to discuss his planned meeting and cautioned him that the Taliban had recently carried off a deception operation up north where they were supposedly surrendering but instead mounted an attack. We told Shirzai that if he still wanted to meet the Taliban commander, he should position a large force at the site well in advance of the scheduled meeting. Shirzai still believed there was a chance he could negotiate the Taliban surrender and wanted to go through with the meeting. No Americans accompanied him, but Hank loaned him some night vision goggles to take along.

Just after dark, Shirzai's force moved down the valley to the appointed meeting spot. A few hours later, they returned and Shirzai gave us his report. His force had arrived well in advance of the meeting and took up defensive positions. Only minutes later, a convoy of Taliban trucks came down the valley. They had stopped some distance before reaching the site and off-loaded the trucks. The Taliban force had spread out and was advancing toward the meeting site. Believing the Taliban were deploying for an attack, Shirzai's men opened up on them and a short firefight ensued; the Taliban retreated.

There would be no more negotiations.

The following morning we met with Shirzai to plan our next steps. It was out in the open on top of the hill near the mud house. We sat in a circle on Afghan carpets with our maps spread out in front of us. In keeping with the plan we had hatched in Jacobabad, we proposed to Shirzai that we go to Spin Boldak first and then move down Highway 4 to Kandahar.

Shirzai pointed out that there were lots of Taliban in Spin Boldak, plus we would have to fight our way through the nearby Taliban garrison to get there. He counter-proposed that we completely avoid Spin Boldak and the Taliban garrison and head straight across the desert for the village of Takhteh-Pol, which sat astride Highway 4 two-thirds of the way to Kandahar from Spin Boldak. There was a small Taliban garrison there, Shirzai said, but if we captured the village, we would cut the main road between Kandahar and Spin Boldak, and thus block al-Qa'ida's primary escape route to Pakistan from southern Afghanistan.

Shirzai's proposal made sense. We were far less interested in capturing Spin Boldak than in controlling Highway 4 to stop the movement of al-Qa'ida. We all agreed; Takhteh-Pol would be our first objective, and plans were made to depart the base camp before dawn the next morning.

That night, figuring it might be my last opportunity to get clean for a while, I decided to take advantage of a bathhouse that Shirzai had set up for us. It was located in a small building a couple hundred meters further up the ridge from the mud house where we were lodged. Inside the bathhouse I found a low wooden platform about a square meter in size that was meant to serve as the washing station. In the house was a fireplace with a small fire already burning that served to heat a pot of water. I moved the water next to the platform and after stripping down I stepped up on the platform and doused myself with the exquisitely warm water using a large ladle that was lying there. While the bath facilities fell short of 5 star luxury, all things considered, they were pretty damn good.

25

Wagons, Ho!

It WAS THE 22ND of November and we were up well before light. The rest of the ODA had arrived by helicopter during the night, an event I had witnessed from afar with the aid of night vision goggles. Standing on a hillside I could see the helicopter descend into the valley, the sound of its rotors low but audible and its dim silhouette visible despite the green and grainy visual effect of the goggles. With the ODA team members' safe arrival, our complement was complete, and everyone was anticipating our imminent departure from the base camp. It was our next big step.

Our means of transport would be an odd mix of vehicles. Shirzai had his big Land Cruiser for himself, Khalil, and a couple of his security guys. The Americans and some of the fighters were to ride in dual cab Hi-Lux Toyota four-wheel drive pickups. These vehicles were "thin-skinned," meaning they had no armor protection. A few fighters would be mounted on scrawny-looking motorcycles, but the bulk of the force would ride in stake-bodied trucks. A final unfortunate few were consigned to make the journey riding on flatbed trailers pulled by farm tractors. When the convoy finally got underway, which proved to be highly problematic, it was a spectacle to behold.

The plan that morning called for everyone to take their vehicle to the fuel supply point to top off their gas tanks, and then form into a convoy heading south down the valley. A gas truck-trailer rig parked at the edge of the dry riverbed served as the fuel supply point.

Very quickly we discovered that there was no gas in the gas trailer. Left unguarded during the previous couple of days, the gas had been stolen. This put a huge dent in our departure plans. Shirzai sent for another gas truck but it took many hours to arrive. Additional organizational problems ensued one after the other, and the confused situation quickly moved beyond a "herding cats" scenario to the level of a stampede. We did not break camp until mid-afternoon.

Our convoy route took us south down the Shin Naray Valley for several kilometers. We passed the landing zone where we had arrived, and then came upon the site of the firefight, but there were no Taliban around. We were driving on what barely qualified as a dirt road, more like a faint track in the dry riverbed, and were forced to move slowly. As we turned westerly and began our ascent out of the valley, one of the big trucks almost overturned trying to traverse an eroded part of the steep road. The occupants spilled out of the sharply angled truck, and it took some time to get it righted and on its way.

Once clear of the valley, we found ourselves on an open plain. Vast and featureless, it offered us unobstructed views. It seemed that if our binoculars had been just a bit more powerful we would have been able to see Kandahar in the faint distance.

My place in the convoy was directly behind Shirzai's Land Cruiser. As the day progressed its dust caked image became burned into my visual cortex like a television test pattern. Every hour or two, at least one vehicle broke down, requiring that we stop until the repair was made.

Day turned to night and we drove until around 1:00 a.m., finally reaching our overnight bivouac, a large, walled compound that belonged to a friend of Shirzai. We slept indoors in our sleeping bags in small alcove-like rooms along a hallway lit by candles burning on the floor. Like the first night we spent in the Shin Naray Valley, the atmosphere was almost romantic if you overlooked the guns, gear, and bearded, smelly men, not to mention the total absence of women.

We pulled out of the compound before light the next morning and resumed our dirt road trek. Not long after the sun rose we reached a tiny village, and Shirzai stopped to get some face time with prospective constituents. While we waited we stomped our insulated, boot-clad feet in vain attempts to keep them warm while the village children walked around laughing and smiling, wearing nothing on their feet but plastic flip-flops. As a crowd of villagers pressed around Shirzai, he handed out money to them like candy at Halloween in hopes of winning their allegiance. It was really no different from politics anywhere else, just more honest and direct. We continued on.

Our speed was a little faster than the day before, but vehicle breakdowns continued to plague the convoy. We were in Taliban territory, and as a general rule we did not want to leave anyone behind to fix a vehicle for fear they would be captured or killed. Accordingly, a lot of valuable time was lost waiting for vehicles to be repaired. Of necessity, exceptions were occasionally made, but when a vehicle had to be left behind for repairs, a security element of fighters remained with it.

During one repair stop, Khalil came back from Shirzai's vehicle and offered up a big bag of little, round nuts for a snack. I grabbed a handful. They were tasty so I ate some more.

"What are these things?"

"Opium seeds."

I guess Khalil could tell by the look on my face that I was concerned.

"Don't worry. It's the leaves of the plant that can mess you up; the seeds don't do anything."

Fortunately this turned out to be true, and I relaxed in the knowledge that I would not have to sweat the drug use question on my next polygraph.

Early in the afternoon the advance element of Shirzai's fighters encountered Taliban—two guys napping in a pickup. Under questioning, they said they were from the local area and were supposed to be guarding the road. They appeared to be low-level members with little information to tell us. The only things of value they had were their pickup truck and guns, which we took. They were given some water and turned loose, and our convoy pushed on in the direction of Takhteh-Pol.

26

The Longest Night

Late IN THE AFTERNOON we pulled into a defensive perimeter for the night. Surrounded by low hills forming a bowl-like configuration, the spot for our bivouac was excellent. Shirzai's fighters occupied the hills, which offered us views for miles around in any direction. Our command post, consisting of my pickup truck, Shirzai's Land Cruiser, and Hank's truck, was set up in the center of the bowl.

Shirzai immediately dispatched a reconnaissance element mounted in Toyota pickups to check out the route to Takhteh-Pol, now only several kilometers away. Several members of the ODA accompanied Shirzai's recon element.

As the sun set and the shadows lengthened, wind gusts kicked up small eddies of dust that danced across the basin we occupied. At dusk the temperature began to fall and some of Shirzai's fighters who had fallen behind earlier in the day straggled in. They reported that word was out among the local populace, which included the Taliban, that there was an anti-Taliban force in the area. Soon, our observation posts started reporting that there were convoys of vehicles headed toward us from three directions. As the temperature continued to drop and the darkness and winds increased, a general sense of foreboding set in.

I climbed up on a hill and through my binoculars saw headlights from two convoys in the distance. They were still many kilometers away, but they were a concern. The fact they were convoys pointed to them likely being Taliban. Coalition bombing policy was that if a convoy was on the road at night, unless identified otherwise, it could be considered a target. If the convoys continued to move once it was dark, they would be fair game.

Concern about the convoys coming our way grew as Shirzai was not expecting any volunteers. The light was all but gone when I heard a couple of shots out beyond our perimeter. It was not clear who fired them. A couple of minutes later something streaked overhead and impacted in the dry riverbed inside the perimeter.

"An RPG dud," an American nearer to the riverbed called out.

A couple of other shots crackled in the distance, but it was impossible to determine what was going on. My guess was that some trigger-happy Shirzai fighter was responsible, but the RPG round coming into our perimeter gave me pause.

About this time, Hank walked over to me and said that he was taking one of Shirzai's fighters and going up on the hillside. He took the SOFLAM laser designator with him. He looked completely relaxed and in his element. *This guy knows what he's doing*, I thought. No more than 30 minutes later, Hank was at work as the sounds of distant explosions could be heard as fast-movers began to hit one of the convoys.

At about the same time, a radio call came in from the recon element. They had run into Taliban on the hills just outside Takhteh-Pol and were taking fire and had called in close air support. About 20 minutes later I spoke by radio to one of the ODA members with the recon element. He told me they had disengaged and were on their way back. They had a few wounded Afghans, but they didn't appear to be in serious condition.

About 10 minutes later, a pickup with one of Shirzai's commanders sped into the perimeter, sharply braking near our command post of trucks. He jumped out of his truck and began shouting. A group of Afghan fighters immediately gathered around him, agitated by what he was saying. I grabbed Khalil and we waded through the throng of fighters to the excited commander. Through Khalil I learned that the commander was saying that the Americans had dropped bombs on his men in the recon element, and they had been wiped out. I told Khalil to tell the commander that I had already spoken with the senior American with the recon element and his fighters had not been wiped out, but there were a few slightly wounded who were being brought back. Hearing this, the commander seemed to settle down, and the mob of fighters that had formed around him dispersed.

Afterward, I learned that bombs had indeed struck in the immediate vicinity of the fighters, as in the darkness they and the Taliban forces had gotten mixed in with one another. When the close air support was called in, the bombs fell among both Shirzai's men and the Taliban.

A few minutes after the episode with Shirzai's agitated commander, the recon element began to return to the bivouac. A nervous Afghan on the perimeter lit up the first pickup with AK fire. It was carrying the SF members, but fortunately no one was hit. A bullet did cut the hydraulic brake line for the right front wheel, however, and from that moment through the next couple of weeks every time the brakes were applied, the pickup would careen to the left. It provided some comic relief during our convoy movements.

The wounded arrived in the other pickups and were driven to our command post. The fighters lifted them out of the trucks and laid them at my feet like human offerings, which in a sense I suppose they were. The SF medic and another ODA member came over and started assessing the wounds. Strangely, not one of the men was bleeding. After questioning them through interpreters we learned they had been very close to where the bombs fell, and the concussive force of the explosions had blown them down a hill. The medic assessed that they were in psychological shock, but they did not appear to have any physical wounds. He told the Afghans to keep the casualties warm and lying down for the next few hours. They picked them up and carried them away.

Hank continued to work through the night with the SOFLAM, keeping approaching vehicles at bay. The temperature became very cold, and the wind continued to blow. It was the coldest night I would spend in Afghanistan, and one of the longest.

My communications window for submitting Foxtrot's daily verbal situation reports to Headquarters was at 2:00 a.m. Gary set up the radio for me, and I made contact with a Headquarters officer who I let myself imagine was probably sitting comfortably in her chair in the middle of the afternoon back at Langley sipping on a soy latte from Starbucks. I didn't recognize her voice and she told me she was new. We exchanged pleasantries and I started dictating my already prepared report. Normally this would be sent in written form, but I still didn't have the gear I needed for that. She had just enough of an Asian accent that I was having difficulty understanding what she said to me over the less than optimal communications link. It was a frustrating situation. Then, right in the middle of my dictation—KABOOM!!! Hank had just called in the closest strike of the night, from the powerful sound of it, right on the other side of the hill where I was huddled with the radio.

"What was that? Did you drop your coffee cup or something?" she innocently asked.

After the call, I walked back to the command post to try to get some sleep. Several Americans were in the back of the pickups curled up in their sleeping bags. Others were inside the truck cabs. There was no room for me in either place. I rolled out my bag and a foam pad on the cold ground, crawled inside, and finally fell asleep to the sound of the howls of the wind.

27

The Longest Day

Early THE NEXT MORNING, and still tired from the previous night, we pulled out of our perimeter and drove toward Takhteh-Pol. After only a short distance we stopped at the edge of an elevated plateau overlooking a broad expanse of ground that led to the hills that stood between Takhteh-Pol and us. These were the same hills where our recon element had gotten into the firefight with the Taliban the night before. Looking it over with binoculars, I could see several vehicles still moving around the Taliban positions, and we decided to call in air strikes before crossing the open ground in daylight.

Within a few minutes, high-flying fast-movers arced overhead dropping ordnance, taking their cues from a young redheaded sergeant who directed them by radio to the targets. The sergeant was confident in his commands, to the point of seeming a bit cocky, given the rap-like staccato cadence he used when talking with the pilots. Whatever the case, he was getting the job done and he seemed to like what he was doing.

By this time the white sun had driven us out of our fleeces, and we basked in its warmth. From our ringside seats, we watched the awesome display of aerial firepower like we might watch fireworks on the 4th of July.

After several strikes, the jets were called off and Shirzai ordered two pickup loads of fighters to reconnoiter the Taliban line of defense. From our vantage point at the lip of the plateau, we watched as the trucks slowly made their way down to the open plain below and then barrel across it, side by side with contrails of dust streaming from their tires. As they raced away, the pickups slowly started to angle away from each other forming a "V" pattern as one headed for the right side of where the Taliban had been and the other for the left. With serrated-peaked mountains in the far distance providing a panoramic backdrop, it was a striking and dramatic scene.

Soon the reconnaissance parties reported the Taliban fighters were gone. We climbed into our trucks and began our own descent down the side of the plateau and then sped across the flat expanse toward Takhteh-Pol.

On the far side of the plain we passed through a tiny collection of little mud homes near where the bombing had taken place. A middle-aged Afghan man stood by the road near one of the homes. One hand was over his heart, the other motioning to us as we rolled by.

"Maybe he is inviting us in for tea," someone joked.

But we had no time for the man, and we laughed and rolled on by.

A couple of kilometers more and the convoy stopped.

"What's up?" I asked Gary who was driving.

"Must be Highway 4."

Having traveled on dirt roads for two days I was imagining what the grand highway would look like. Curious to see it, I asked Gary to pull our truck around the stopped vehicles to get a look. From what we could see, it did not look much different than the roads we had traveled, with the exception that it was wider and there were stretches of deteriorated pavement here and there. It was also cratered with potholes; some so large a pickup could drive into them and almost disappear from sight.

We were now no more than a kilometer or two from Takhteh-Pol. We suspected that after all the bombing the Taliban would have fled the village, and we sent some fighters in to check it out. Meanwhile, Shirzai instructed his forces to set up a roadblock on the highway and to stop and search any vehicles approaching from the direction of Spin Boldak.

All members of Foxtrot were together at this point and we pulled our pickup over to a low dirt embankment off the road to provide a flanking base of fire should there be problems at the roadblock. As we watched, I decided to ask Gary about something I had noticed over the last couple of days.

"No offense, Gary, I'm not complaining about your company, but it seems like you or Mike are always hovering around me. What's up with that?"

"You don't know?" he asked incredulously. "We're acting as your bodyguards. It was part of the justification used to get authorization for us to deploy with Foxtrot."

I thought that was really funny.

"Well, forget that. Thanks for your services, but you guys have enough to worry about without worrying about me."

After a few minutes I walked over to talk to Shirzai who was parked nearby. I looked back to make sure neither Gary nor Mike were following me. They weren't. My message had been received.

Up until this point, I had generally taken a back seat during tactical discussions with Shirzai concerning engagements with the Taliban, letting Hank and his ODA be the military advisors since that is what an ODA is trained to do. I believed that role, along with calling in close air support, was their primary task. But now that we were at Highway 4 and almost on the doorstep of Kandahar, I knew our chance of engaging al-Qa'ida members in the next few hours was probably very good. When all was said and done, that was what Foxtrot was there to do as a field element of CIA's Counterterrorist Center. With this in mind, through Khalil I told Shirzai that as soon as we secured the village, he needed to set up and maintain roadblocks on both sides of town. I reminded him our primary targets were members of al-Qa'ida and that his men should detain any foreigner they came across.

Word came back that the village was clear of the Taliban and we moved in. My first order of business was to check out the roadblock that Shirzai had set up on the western end of the village. As I walked along Highway 4, which at that stretch was just a dirt street that passed through the center of the tiny village, I saw some of Shirzai's men getting ready to hoist the green Afghan flag on a pole that previously held a Taliban flag. I pulled out my disposable Kodak and snapped a picture. It wasn't the flag raising at Iwo Jima, but it was still a pretty cool moment.

At the roadblock, Shirzai's fighters already had stopped a couple of vehicles. One was an old stake-bodied truck, the other was a beat up sedan. No al-Qa'ida, just some farmers and a local passing by.

Satisfied that the roadblocks were functioning, I walked back towards the small, walled compound that had previously belonged to the Taliban. It would now serve as our command post. Near the compound I ran into Hank.

"Hey, you shouldn't be walking around out here. It's dangerous and we need to keep a low profile," he said.

He was right, of course, but I needed to see for myself that the roadblocks were up and operating. Now that I had done that I could get out of sight.

"OK, I'm heading over to the compound right now."

The former Taliban compound was relatively small, with one larger building and a few other smaller ones. A wall about 7 feet high surrounded the entire complex. We moved into the buildings and set up our communications gear, as we believed we would probably be there for a few days.

In the small building Foxtrot occupied, we found dishes with pieces of partially eaten bread and teacups half-filled, all evidence of a hasty departure. I imagined the "breakfast-interrupted" scene that must have transpired earlier that morning. Black turbaned Taliban enjoying their naan and chai when—KABOOM—they hear the first bomb explode only a couple of kilometers away. They pick up and get out of Dodge, or Takhteh-Pol as it were.

We all pitched in and searched the compound, anticipating booby-traps. Found in the basement of the main building were all kinds of ordnance, but mostly mortar and RPG rounds. We didn't like having an arsenal right in the middle of our compound so Shirzai ordered his men to take it away to a safer place, and we watched them as they carefully carried it out the front gate.

An hour or two later, I spotted Khalil quickly striding toward me.

"An Arab has been captured at the roadblock. Come quick!"

I went out the compound gate with him and walked across the open area toward Highway 4 only a short distance away. As we approached the road, a small mob of fighters suddenly came around the corner of a building about 50 feet away, gesturing and yelling as they hurriedly moved toward us. For the first couple of seconds, I could not figure out just what I was looking at. I knew they were friendlies, but something about the scene instinctively put me on edge, and I tightened my grip on my AK-47. Then I saw the prisoner. One of the Afghans had him by the collar of his shirt and was pulling him along. He was unsecured otherwise. By the time I had spotted him, he already had seen me. Directly in front of him and in the open, I was an obvious Westerner.

As soon as our eyes met, he reached down and violently tried to yank an AK-47 from the hands of an Afghan walking beside him. At that point, my mind went into hyper-focus and things slowed down. I watched as what seemed like a slow-motion struggle ensued as the Arab continued to try to wrest control of the rifle from the Afghan. At one point, the owner's grip slipped and the Arab grabbed the rifle again, this time by the barrel as he continued to struggle mightily to take control of it. The Afghan stepped out in front of the Arab and tried to sling him off the rifle, but the man still tugged violently at the gun. I could plainly see the determination in his face—he wanted that rifle. After two or three seconds more the Afghan squeezed off a burst of about five rounds point blank into the Arab's body. At almost the same instant another Afghan standing behind him opened up on him as well.

Still in a hyper-focused state I could see the bullets pass out of his body front and back, popping and snapping his loose fitting clothing as they tore through him. He went down instantly and hard—like a ton of bricks, a cliché that described his fall perfectly—and I knew he was dead before he hit the ground. The group of Afghans swirled in excitement around his limp body like an ocean tide around a stranded fish on the beach. My perception clicked back into normal speed.

I had zero emotion about the shooting. This surprised me. Had I discovered some heretofore hidden sociopathic trait about myself? I really thought I should have felt something. But I didn't. I was not excited, scared, happy, angry—nothing. I didn't feel any hatred toward the now dead man, even though I was certain he would have killed me if he could have. On the other hand, I didn't feel any sympathy for him either. We had both come to Afghanistan knowing it was dangerous and that we might die. Today he died, tomorrow I might. And that was it.

I turned to Khalil, "Looks like we won't be talking to him."

Khalil nodded and I told him to have the men search the body for any documents and bring them to me.

Khalil relayed my instructions to the fighters and we walked back toward the compound.

"Did you see him try to grab that grenade?" Khalil asked.

"What grenade?"

"You didn't see? He was fighting trying to take a grenade from our guy."

"I saw him trying to take away the rifle, but there wasn't any grenade," I said.

"No. He was after a grenade."

I was shocked that Khalil was saying he had not seen the struggle for the rifle, and instead was saying the fight was over a grenade, which I knew was not the case. How could both of us witness the same event from the same location and have seen things so differently? It was a mystery, and neither of us would give ground on what we believed we had seen.

I had scarcely returned to the compound following the shooting when a wounded fighter was brought in. He was gut shot with two AK-47 rounds through his abdomen and was groaning in pain. He had been shot at one of the roadblocks when two al-Qa'ida members decided to fight it out. They both were dead. We were told the wounded Afghan was Shirzai's first cousin and the two were very close. He was carried into the building Shirzai was using for his headquarters, and the medics went to work on him. They were not hopeful for his survival.

A little while later, I was standing in the compound near the front gate when an Afghan civilian appeared. He was the same man that was waving to us earlier as we drove toward Takhteh-Pol. He had a little girl in his arms, his daughter. She was about seven or eight years old. She was wounded from one of the bombs that had been dropped on the Taliban defensive line. The wound was a deep facial cut, so deep you could see the light color of her cheekbone peeking through the gash in her caramel skin. She was not crying but was curled tightly into her father's arms, terrified.

We carried her into the building where the medics were still working on Shirzai's cousin. One of them started to tend to her wound and she began to scream.

I went outside and sat down on the front steps to make some notes about what I would need to include in the next situation report. As I wrote, the little girl's screams and the groans of the wounded Afghan fighter mixed together into a discordant duet of pain, the effect of which was to obliterate any concern of mine that I was an unfeeling sociopath.

The little girl's wound was stitched up but the medic was not happy with his handiwork. Concerned that the wound would leave a nasty scar, we gave the father some money and arranged for a hired car to take them to Spin Boldak. There was a hospital there with doctors who could maybe improve on the medic's stitching technique.

The father did not appear to be angry with us, which amazed me. I would have been angry if it were my daughter that had been injured by our bombs and probably scarred for life. But no, he seemed okay about it, not one glimmer of hatred in his eyes, at least none that I could detect. He seemed appreciative of the medical help and money we gave him, and he picked up the little girl and carried her away.

Shortly after dark, Shirzai's fighters brought in two Arabs captured at the roadblock on the east side of Takhteh-Pol. The fighters had learned their lessons, and the prisoners were blindfolded and bound in chains. Inside the car that one of the Arabs, a Yemeni, was driving, a trunk full of SA-7 anti-aircraft missiles was discovered.

I watched as the prisoners were silently searched by Gary, Mike, and a couple members of the ODA, and then were placed in special plastic handcuffs and put under Afghan guard in separate mud buildings. None of Shirzai's fighters spoke Arabic and of the Americans, only Mike knew the language but not at a level needed to conduct an interrogation.

When he was captured, the Yemeni had in his possession a small walkie-talkie radio, and we listened to it as someone speaking in Arabic pleadingly called for him like a lost puppy. It was clear the caller was worried about him and continued to call for him over the next couple of days. The radio signal was very clear and strong as if the caller was close by, which seemed unlikely, and we suspected al-Qa'ida had set up radio repeaters along Highway 4 to keep in touch with its members traveling between Kandahar and Pakistan.

If we were to have any hope of obtaining any useful information from the two prisoners, they needed to undergo a professional interrogation in Arabic as soon as possible. Hank and I conferred and he put in a request to 5th Special Forces Group to have an Arabic-speaking interrogator flown down to Takhteh-Pol. It took a couple of days but they sent us one. Although Mark and I looked on, the Army guys were in charge of the interrogation.

The Yemeni was of most interest to us given his carload of surface-to-air missiles. During the interrogation, he claimed to have no association with al-Qa'ida, and said he worked in Afghanistan for a particular NGO, which we knew al-Qa'ida used as a cover in Afghanistan. The prisoner had no explanation for driving toward Kandahar in a car loaded with surface-to-air missiles.

When the interrogator left we requested he take the prisoners with him, as we were not set up to hold prisoners for any extended period of time. Reluctantly, and after some back and forth communications with 5th SF Group Headquarters, he left with the prisoners on a helicopter.

*   *   *

The Yemini captured turned out to be Salim Hamdan, the personal driver and bodyguard for Osama Bin Laden. He would be transferred to the U.S. military base at Guantanamo, Cuba, and his case was to be the first to be tried under the military tribunal system. Under appeal, the case known as Hamdan vs. Rumsfeld, ultimately reached the U.S. Supreme Court, which ruled in Hamdan's favor and forced the military to change the tribunal procedures. Hamdan was eventually convicted of terrorism charges but was given credit for time served. He was released a few months after his conviction and returned to Yemen in 2014.

28

Bad News

On THE FOLLOWING DAY Shirzai's men killed four more al-Qa'ida members at the roadblocks. None were captured. It was apparent al-Qa'ida preferred martyrdom to surrendering. No surprise there.

Out of concern that the roadblocks and our command post could become targets of car bombs, we collectively agreed that no vehicles would be allowed to pass through Takhteh-Pol going in either direction. The implementation of this decision effectively stopped all traffic traveling between Kandahar and Spin Boldak on Highway 4. The roadblocks became just what their name implied and primitive signs were put out to warn drivers there was no passage, and if they approached they would be fired on.

Shirzai's wounded cousin remained in critical condition and would die if we did not get him better care. The policy was that we could treat Afghans on site but could not medically evacuate them to U.S. facilities. We requested an exception to policy and crossed our fingers.

That afternoon I received a message on my satellite pager to call CTC/SO. I called the office using secure voice communications, wondering what was up. The answer was not anything I had anticipated. My Headquarters contact told me that Mike Spann, a CIA paramilitary officer operating up north in the Mazar-e-Sharif area was missing and presumed dead, which if true, meant he was the first American killed in Afghanistan. I didn't know Mike, but the news stung me just the same.

"Everyone at Headquarters is shocked that this has happened," she said.

Really? I was surprised that anyone at Headquarters, at least if they worked in CTC/SO, could be "shocked" by this tragic news. Upset, yes. Shocked, no. Didn't they know what was going on here? Didn't they understand?

"Don't be shocked again if you get some more bad news before this is all over," I said, somewhat angered and frustrated by what I perceived to be an inexplicable naiveté at Headquarters. "This is very much an uncontrolled environment out here and anything can happen at any time."

I really wasn't exactly sure why this exchange concerning the news of Mike's death had riled me so. I guess I just thought they should have understood that something like this was going to happen.

Later that same day, I received the long-awaited word that the CIA paramilitary officers were on their way to join Foxtrot, bringing the much-needed communications gear with them. I was told there were five of them inbound, which I believed was too large a group. We were living in tight conditions and were not in the best tactical situation. To our west, many thousands of enemy forces were still in Kandahar and to our east thousands more were in Spin Boldak. Moreover, the real work for us would not start until we got into the city of Kandahar and began to hunt for al-Qa'ida members and any exploitable intelligence that could be found. Given those factors, I did not believe any more Agency lives than necessary should be put at risk.

The paramilitary team was coming through the U.S. base at Karsi Khanabad, Uzbekistan, so I called up to our flight operations center and told them to only send two of the paramilitary officers to Takhteh-Pol, and that if possible, the other three should remain in Karsi Khanabad until Foxtrot reached Kandahar, and they could join us then. The person on the other end of the line gave me a "roger," and I thought it was a done deal.

Around midnight the following night as the paramilitary team was flying in on a helicopter, I found out that all five PM officers were onboard. I was not happy with this news.

Shortly before the helicopter's arrival, Gary and I walked out to the landing zone just outside the village. Gary expertly marked the landing zone by attaching a small infrared light to a long piece of parachute cord, and when the helo came in range he began to swing the light over his head in a circle that grew larger and larger as he slowly fed out more of the cord. The pilots with their IR goggles spotted the light and brought the blacked-out helo down, creating a total brown-out on the ground. I had goggles on to protect my eyes from the blowing sand, but I did not have any night vision goggles. Gary did, however, and he grabbed me by the shoulder and we ran together toward the helo. It was a huge exercise in trust for me because I could not see anything, and I knew there were powerful rotors cutting through the darkness that we were running directly toward. Earlier in my career I had participated in team building exercises where you fell backwards into the arms of your colleagues trusting them to catch you. That exercise amounted to child's play compared to this. Gary delivered me safely to the bird, and I climbed up the tail ramp. Inside the cabin there was some faint light so I was able to see. I grabbed the closest man I saw.

"Who is the senior officer," I shouted into his ear because of the noise.

"I am," he shouted back.

"I only want two guys who know the commo system the best to stay. The other three will have to go back."

It was a hard decision for me to send anyone back. I, of all people, understood how badly those men wanted to be there. Additionally, flying around in a helicopter in Afghanistan was risky in and of itself, and after just arriving and taking that risk, I'm sending them right back up in the air. *They were going to hate me.*

John, the senior officer, simply said, "OK," and he relayed the word to the other team members. I saw the dismayed looks on their faces. *Yep, they hated me.*

John designated another PM officer named Pat to come with him. As the Helo sat on the ground with its engines running, the team quickly repacked the hard shell Pelican equipment boxes, being careful to make sure all the comms gear was transferred to the boxes that would remain in Takhteh-Pol. After a couple of minutes we offloaded the helicopter, and it immediately lifted off. Within an hour Foxtrot had full communications and our first written report was sent advising Headquarters of the arrival of John and Pat. Having the proper communications gear was a huge upgrade to Foxtrot team. It meant that for the first time we would be able to send and receive written CIA reporting.

Over the next few days I learned how fortunate Foxtrot was to have the two new officers on the team. John had spent an entire career in Delta Force before coming to the Agency. He was an imposing figure with a taciturn personality that conveyed the message that he did not put up with any bullshit. Even though there had been nothing from Headquarters on the subject, given John's exceptional military background and paramilitary experience, I assumed he was supposed to take my place as Foxtrot team leader. When he said nothing about it, I asked him if this was the case. "No", he replied, "you're it."

John's partner, Pat, was an Air Force veteran. Smaller in stature than John, he was soft-spoken and generally low key, but there was an underlying toughness about him that reminded me of a Clint Eastwood character from a western. As I would learn, Pat did have some volatility in his personality if the wrong button was pushed, and he was not afraid to call a spade a spade.

With the commo gear and the two of them on board, I felt like Foxtrot was now a full-up team.

*   *   *

Approval for the medical evacuation of Shirzai's wounded cousin did come through. He was flown to Germany and then eventually to the U.S., where after a year of medical treatment he recovered and then returned to Afghanistan.

29

Takhteh-Pol Days

The CONSOLIDATION OF THE Takhteh-Pol area and the blocking of Highway 4 had been our immediate preoccupation for the first two to three days since Foxtrot entered the village, but the capture of Kandahar remained our primary objective. This was true for Echo team as well, which was pushing southward with Hamid Karzai's forces toward Kandahar from the Tarin Kowt area

Kandahar was not far from Takhteh-Pol, only a little over an hour's drive, but standing in our way was an estimated 400 determined and dug-in al-Qa'ida and Taliban fighters who occupied the Kandahar airport that sat alongside Highway 4 east of the city. The capture of the airport would be an important key to the taking of the city. An immediate ground attack by Shirzai's forces against the airport would likely be unacceptably costly in terms of casualties, and we ruled it out for the time being. Instead we decided to lay siege to the airport using ODA-directed airstrikes, providing time to soften up its defenses.

Toward this end, on December 1st, Shirzai's forces, despite meeting some resistance, pushed out the western security perimeter around Takhteh-Pol and established a strongpoint at a concrete bridge on Highway 4 that spanned the dry riverbed of the Arghastan River. The bridge was only about two or three kilometers from the main airport complex and had line-of-sight across generally open terrain. The ODA set up an observation post at the bridge and began to call in air strikes, rotating ODA members back to Takhteh-Pol for rest purposes. Takhteh-Pol was about a 25-minute drive from the bridge, and our compound there continued to serve as the command post.

A force of Shirzai's fighters was still maintained to the east of the village to guard against an attack from the direction of Spin Boldak, while other security and observation elements were scattered around at key points of what had become a very large perimeter covering many miles. Shirzai's force was not large enough to cover it completely, so unavoidably there were holes in the defensive line, if it could be called a line at all, and it was possible an enemy force could slip past to attack our command post at Takhteh-Pol. Despite these deficiencies, priority had to go to keeping the bulk of Shirzai's fighters in the vicinity of the bridge to deter an attack against the ODA'S observation point which was calling in a rain of death on the enemy on a near continuous basis.

As strikes against the airport got underway, we settled into a routine at the compound. One of the constants was that there was always at least one American awake 24 hours a day. At night this took the form of a one-hour rotating shift. The ODA members were not included due to their own rotation schedule for calling airstrikes. This left the members of Foxtrot, and three or four military Special Ops personnel who joined Foxtrot a couple days after we moved into Takhteh-Pol, to keep watch. Everyone got at least one shift a night and usually one person had to pull two.

Reflective of the generally relaxed and democratic leadership style I used with this team of experienced professionals, any one of whom could have done as good of a job, maybe better, as team leader, I proposed our shifts be for two hours. A longer shift would mean everyone would get a full night's sleep every other day. Unfortunately, my wisdom was lost on the team and I was voted down.

During the night watch, a fire was kept with a pot of coffee or tea gurgling over it. Each one of us, in turn, sat by the fire, usually wearing a black fleece jacket and baseball cap. We were kept company by the pilots' chatter on the radio we monitored as air strikes were carried out, and we would listen to the corresponding deep rumbling of the ordnance detonating in the distance.

Another constant, at least for me, was that I was armed at all times. Even at the command post I always carried the Glock-19 on my belt. At night I slept with it by my side and with my AK-47 leaning against the wall an arm's reach away. I, and most of the other Americans, took these precautions due to the constant threat of possible attack on Takhteh-Pol by al-Qa'ida or Taliban forces. But there was also a real concern of an insider attack against us by one or more of the Afghan fighters with whom we were working. We were not in a position to vet any of them and were completely relying on Shirzai's assessment that we could trust our lives to the armed Afghans who were constantly around us.

One afternoon Mike, myself, and a couple of others were outside in the compound courtyard when a deafening barrage of AK-47 fire erupted a few feet away on the other side of the compound wall. Having no idea of what was happening, I ducked into the small building where I slept and grabbed my AK-47 and took a defensive position in the doorway, thinking the firing indicated we were under attack. Mike was still in the courtyard and had moved up against the wall opposite from where the firing was going on. Very bravely, he lifted his head momentarily above the wall to see what was happening and then lowered it, shaking it as he did. We weren't under attack—the Afghans had just decided to test their weapons and hadn't advised any one inside the compound of their plans. Although it was a false alarm, it reinforced for me that we always had to be ready for the unexpected, and that meant being armed at all times and places. The incident also highlighted the fact that the Afghan force we were with was not very disciplined and not well trained in the safe handling of weapons. On several occasions when there was no evident threat, I saw Afghans walking about with their fingers on the triggers of their AK's. Muzzle control was an even bigger problem, with the barrels of their rifles often being carelessly slung about pointing in one unsafe direction or the other. I actually believed that the chances were as good or greater that I or another member of Foxtrot would be accidently wounded or killed by one of Shirzai's men as by any deliberate attack by al-Qa'ida or the Taliban.

* * *

Every few nights a detail was formed to go out into the desert to receive a parachute resupply of guns, ammo, and other equipment. Though it was counter-intuitive, owing to the provisions of Title 50 authorities, CIA was responsible for the provision of lethal material, and the Special Forces team was responsible for non-lethal supplies.

One night, among the supplies received, were two big bags of horse feed. Some teams up north did have horses, and I was a little jealous about that. Having grown up with horses, I had this romantic idea about using them in Foxtrot's activities in the South. But the only steeds we had were the dual-cab, 4-wheel drive kind, and they didn't eat grain. As was standard practice, we sent a routine message back listing the supplies received. Before I pushed the send button to release the report, unbeknownst to me, one of the team members had added a special parenthetical note next to the entry about the bags of feed to insure Headquarters understood Foxtrot was a non-equestrian team. It read: "We don't have any fucking horses." It was the first and only time in my entire career that I had ever seen the "F" word in a CIA cable, as profanity is strictly prohibited in official correspondence. So I was taken aback to see it as plain as day in a cable that I had just released to my Headquarters, though I couldn't help but laugh.

Obscene cable or not, I was actually glad we had the horse feed. The sweet smell of the grain, and the sight and feel of the rough burlap bags provoked boyhood memories of feeding our horses using a red Folgers coffee can to scoop the grain out of a bag identical to the ones stacked against the compound wall. As the days passed, I sometimes found myself coming up with reasons to walk past them, just so I could inhale the nostalgic fragrance. In some ways the smell seemed more powerful in reminding me of my youth spent in New Mexico than the sight of the azure Afghan sky and the brown earth beneath it.

*   *   *

After John's arrival he became Foxtrot team's de facto commo officer. As with everything else he did, he was very organized and strict about how things were accomplished. One day I was trying to draft a cable to Headquarters on the team laptop and had trouble logging in with the password. After one too many attempts, the computer's security feature kicked in and locked up the computer. John, who I had already learned did not take fools lightly, was perturbed by my technical ineptitude.

"From now on, I will log into the computer. You don't touch it until I say it is ready."

I felt like I was back in the Army as a brand new second lieutenant, and John was my platoon sergeant trying to protect me from myself. And just like I did with my platoon sergeant, I followed John's direction.

Pat also had a similar experience with John involving the computer, and he did not take it as well as I had. Pat came to me furious, complaining about the way John had talked down to him.

"I swear I will deck that asshole if he pulls that shit again," he said.

Fortunately, it never came to fisticuffs between the two, but it could have, as I had no doubt that Pat would be true to his word. And John, well—John was John.

*   *   *

Late one afternoon a cable came in from Uzbekistan. I knew the chief there, and he was forwarding an intelligence report that was sent to his base but not to Foxtrot team. The report said that the Taliban's II Corps based in Kandahar was planning to launch a surprise attack against Takhteh-Pol that very night.

I had to shake my head. Foxtrot team occupied Takhteh-Pol and yet no one had thought to put us down on the dissemination line of the report—this despite the fact that all the other CIA teams in Afghanistan, none even close to Takhteh-Pol, had received it. It was not the first time that something like this had happened, and at times it seemed to me that Foxtrot was the "forgotten team." I had to believe that at least part of the reason for this mistake was that we had not been up on the communications net sending and receiving CIA traffic for very long, but still, given the importance of the report—possibly a life and death matter—failing to send the report to Foxtrot team was an egregious error.

We knew our security line was thin, and that a concerted enemy effort, if it was not detected early, could punch through, or depending on its location, just saunter through. We advised Shirzai of the threatened attack. With all his fighters already on the line, all he had left were his Hazara cooks, the only non-Pashtuns among his force, to send out and reinforce the lines.

The Hazaras were of special interest to me. They spoke Dari so when I first learned that there were some of them with Shirzai, I was hopeful I could speak to them using my Farsi, a closely related language. I spoke Farsi at a professional level, however, meaning it was proper Farsi and was intended for an educated audience. The Hazaras with us were illiterate, backcountry people and spoke Dari with a thick colloquial accent. They called my Farsi "Khatab-e-Farsi" (book Farsi). In my attempts to converse with them, they seemed to understand me, but I could understand scarcely a word they said.

They enjoyed our conversations, however, if their outbursts of laughter were any gauge.

That night as I watched the Hazaras march out of the compound to reinforce the line, I saw they had traded their cooking pots and utensils for grenades, AKs, and RPGs, which hung from them like pieces of industrial-sized jewelry. No longer cooks, they had transformed into formidable warriors.

The consensus opinion among the members of Foxtrot team was one of skepticism about the Taliban being able to pull off an attack. Still, our lines were vulnerable, and as a precaution I told everyone to start getting their gear together in case we had to abandon the village *in extremis*. Under this contingency, the plan was to fall back to the defensive position we had occupied the night before we had captured Takhteh-Pol.

As everyone started to go pack their rucksacks, John cautioned that the Afghans were watching, and if they got the idea that the Americans were getting ready to leave, it would weaken their determination to fight. He had a good point, so I modified the plan; we held off packing but made sure we could lay our hands on our gear quickly if we had to move.

Either the intelligence was bad, or the Taliban changed their minds, for there was no attack against Takhteh-Pol that night.

*   *   *

One day, the ODA got a message that their headquarters wanted to send to our location a Special Forces Command and Control Element (CCE) of 15 personnel commanded by a lieutenant colonel. Neither Hank nor myself thought it was a good idea for the same reasons that I had not wanted all five CIA paramilitary officers to join us. It just didn't make sense. In the case of the CCE, what was there to command and control? In all of southern Afghanistan, there were only the two ODA's co-located with Foxtrot and Echo teams, for a total of around 23 Special Forces personnel, and they were doing quite well on their own, thank you. Did they really require a headquarters element to supervise them? To bring that many people into tiny Takhteh-Pol would significantly increase the American presence, making a bigger bulls eye with no discernible mission benefit. With my support, Hank pushed back on the idea and the CCE did not come to Takhteh-Pol, but instead joined the ODA with Echo Team and Karzai.

*   *   *

Mark and I decided to drive out to the observation post on the bridge one morning. We cleared it with Hank, as that was his operational area, and I knew he did not want non-essential personnel hanging around the bridge while his ODA called in airstrikes. At the last minute, one of Shirzai's senior advisors, who we referred to as "Engineer Pashtun," joined us. He mentioned he had to be back in Takhteh-Pol in a couple hours to be present at a meeting with some local tribal elders that Shirzai was hosting. I told him we would get him back in time.

We made the drive on Highway 4 crossing a wide expanse of desert terrain that gently sloped to the bridge over the Arghastan River. The highway was severely deteriorated and most of the way it was simply a dirt road, so movement was slow. Upon arrival at the observation post, we watched as high flying jets were vectored in to drop their bombs on designated targets around the airport complex. I could see a small force of Shirzai's fighters driving forward toward the airfield in pickup trucks. They parked and dismounted the pickups and continued forward on foot to probe the al-Qa'ida defenses. They were a considerable distance away from the bridge, perhaps 1,000 meters or more, but close enough to see without the aid of binoculars. Aircraft were circling overhead ready to provide close air support.

Suddenly, the Afghans began to withdraw, appearing to take fire from unseen enemy positions. The ODA combat controller kneeling on the ground beside us called for close air support to protect their retreat. He craned his neck to look up at the incoming attacking jet.

"No, this is wrong. That bird ain't tracking right," he said.

The jet let loose with machinegun fire and the rounds began chewing up the ground around the Afghan fighters and the pickups.

"Abort, abort, those are friendlies!" he told the attacking aircraft.

We were thinking the worst—that there would be casualties—but we lucked out, or the Afghans lucked out. Miraculously, no one was hit.

After spending a little more time at the bridge I told Mark and Engineer Pashtun that we needed to get back if he was going to make his meeting. As we prepared to leave, the observation post received word from the Afghans that they suspected the enemy might be planning to mount an attack. We waited for a while but could see nothing from our position to help assess the situation. I thought it was unlikely that al-Qa'ida would attempt a direct attack against the bridge as it was broad daylight, generally open terrain, and aircraft were already on station striking targets. I was more concerned that on our return trip our one-pickup convoy would be vulnerable should there actually be an enemy force maneuvering in the area. I told Mark and Engineer Pashtun that we had better get going, and we loaded up and headed back to the village. It was an uneventful trip back to Takhteh-Pol, and we arrived in time for Engineer Pashtun to make his meeting with Shirzai and the local leaders.

Later, Mark approached me and said that he was worried that we could have lost credibility with the ODA by not staying at the bridge given the report of a possible attack. I had not considered it from that perspective at the time, but he had a point. I felt badly that I had not thought about it before if it might have put us in a bad light with the ODA. Although no attack on the bridge occurred, it was a mistake on my part all the same.

* * *

Occasionally, Shirzai's fighters found documents on the bodies of Taliban and al-Qa'ida that had been killed in the bombings or in the firefights that sometimes took place. These were passed on to us for reporting to Headquarters. One day we received a batch of around 15 passports collected from the dead, which was a higher number than usual. In addition to the passports, there were passport-sized photographs of the deceased. It was evident from the photographs that the men were trying to change their appearance from the photos in their passports. Some had shaved their beards or changed their hairstyle, or in some cases, put on or taken off a pair of glasses. My assumption was this had been done in anticipation of using the photographs to obtain other identity documents under false names.

Probably half of the dead were holders of Turkish passports, the others were Saudis or Yeminis, and a couple of them were from Morocco. I was surprised at how young the men were, most no more than their early 20's. As I typed up the identifying data taken from the passports and looked at the photographs of the young men, I wondered about the thought process they went through to arrive at a decision to leave their homelands to come to Afghanistan to fight, and in their cases, to die. They certainly didn't look like fanatic religious ideologues. I suspected some of them had no idea of what they were getting into.

30

Lightning Strikes—Twice

It WAS THE 4TH of December, and John and I were sitting in the compound courtyard on director-style camp chairs, basking in the late afternoon sunshine. John was on a satellite phone talking to Headquarters, while I was taking the opportunity to relax. It was such pleasant weather and the thought occurred to me that if this was a "normal country," people might come stay here for a winter haven. The thought quickly passed as the sounds of more bombing of the airport intruded on my musings.

As John continued his phone conversation, I noticed an unusual little hissing noise mixed in with the sounds of the distant bomb explosions. *Hmm, I've never heard that before.* Then KABOOM! A powerful explosion erupted a couple hundred meters outside the south side of the compound wall. Several other equally powerful explosions followed in rapid succession. John and I jumped up out of our chairs and looked at each other, eyes wide. Like a scene from a movie, John yelled into the phone, "Got to go. We've got incoming! . . . Yeah, really, incoming!"

"Those were rockets, six in total," he said to me.

With 20 years in Delta Force behind him, plus his having been rocketed once during the first Gulf War, I took his word for it. I was amazed that he had kept count.

A few seconds later, we heard the now not-so-funny hissing noise again. We had no foxholes to dive into and the mud house we lived in wasn't going to provide any protection either, even if we could get there in time—which we couldn't. So we just stood there, looking at each other, and I wondered if John's face would be the last thing I would see on this earth. For a lot of reasons, I hoped not.

Once again a volley of six jolting explosions rocked the compound in rapid succession. This time the rockets had flown over us hitting a couple hundred meters to the east, indicating the gunners were adjusting their fire as they tried to bracket our position.

As we waited to see if there would be any more rounds, across the compound Mark stepped out from Shirzai's headquarters building, stood at the top of the concrete steps, and shouted to no one in particular.

"I've been shot at and missed, and I am not putting up with any more bullshit for the rest of my life!" He then turned and walked back inside the building.

Mark's outburst was reminiscent of Churchill's statement that "Nothing in life is so exhilarating as to be shot at without result." If "exhilarating" included learning precisely where the pit of your stomach was located, then Churchill and I were in complete agreement.

But I had another insight on the failed attempt on our lives: *Total strangers have just tried to kill me. Twice. They don't even know me, that I'm really a good guy, and that I have friends and family who love me. It doesn't matter to them. They just want me dead.*

Up to that moment I thought I already understood that about the enemy, but the rockets had taken that abstract thinking and made it concrete and tangible. A moment of clarity had come. Their trying to kill me wasn't personal. It was the opposite: it was completely impersonal.

The artillery rockets also taught me something else: that my equating those rockets with lightning was an accurate analogy, though with one major difference. They don't come out of nowhere—they have a return address.

Almost immediately after the second round of rockets, a report came in from a perimeter lookout who saw the rocket launch site in a small valley. The ODA called for an immediate air strike. As chance would have it, a B-52 was already inbound for a bombing run on Kandahar, and it was only a couple of minutes out. It was diverted and dropped its payload on the rocket launcher. The entire area was turned upside down by the strike. They had fired 12 rockets at us, and we almost instantaneously hit them with an arc light strike. That had to be demoralizing for the enemy.

Before dark a detail went out and searched the area where the rockets hit. They found the motors for the rockets, which enabled us to identify them as 122mm caliber. It was also discovered that the ordnance that had been taken out of our compound and moved to a "safer" place when we first moved in had actually been stacked up against the back wall of the house Foxtrot occupied. Had one of the rockets impacted the pile of ordnance, it would not have gone well for any of us.

We thought we were done with the rocket attacks but the next morning a single rocket struck at us. It impacted 800 to 1,000 meters to the north, kicking up a plume of dust. We learned later that a patrolling jet had spotted the offending mobile rocket launcher and destroyed it with a missile strike.

31

Friendly Fire

The DAY AFTER THE rocket attack on Takhteh-Pol, a message came in advising that Echo team's location had been hit. Three Americans were dead and many others wounded. Two of the dead were members of ODA 574, and a third was from the Special Forces Command and Control Element that had planned to come to Takhteh-Pol, and only recently joined Echo team. Miraculously, no CIA officers from Echo team were killed or injured, but dozens of Hamid Karzai's fighters were, and Karzai himself was slightly wounded.

The initial report said that it was a car bomb attack. Later, we received clarification that it was a U.S. Air Force 500 lb. J-DAM that was dropped directly on the ODA'S observation post. The deadly mistake was due to a procedural error made by one of the members of the SF CCE who was directing the air strikes.

The news of the deaths and injuries stabbed at my heart. I immediately thought of the ODA members I had gotten to know in Jacobabad when I was with Echo team. Among the wounded were Jason, the team leader, and Mag, the intel sergeant, who received a severe head injury. The two dead from the ODA included a young sergeant referred to as "JD" who I did not have the chance to get to know very well, and Dan, the team sergeant. Dan had joined the team at the last minute, just before it had departed from Jacobabad and the only contact I had with him was to shake his hand when we were introduced upon his arrival.

I pictured the guys on Echo team who had escaped the fate of the ODA but who, nonetheless, had to be living through a nightmare. I remembered the day I last saw them, loading their gear in preparation for their infiltration into Afghanistan, and how intensely proud I had felt. Should I have had an inkling that such an enormous tragedy was going to befall them, I think my heart would have burst.

I also had to consider what would have happened if the CCE had come to Foxtrot's location instead of joining Echo team. All those men who were killed and wounded would still have been alive and well. But would the same mistake have been made at our observation post, and would some of the living among us now be dead or wounded? These were imponderable questions, but they nagged at me. I was not keeping a diary, but if I had been I would have written: Impersonal *and* random. These are two things I have learned are true about war.

*   *   *

Back at home, while preparing to go to work my wife heard the news report of the American deaths and injuries in southern Afghanistan. Believing that there was only one team of Americans in the south, she assumed I was with that team, and she feared I may have been among the casualties. She immediately got in touch with a point of contact at CIA who assured that I was safe and had not been with the team.

32

Kandahar

On DECEMBER 6TH, GUESTS from Great Britain arrived at our compound. It was a Royal Navy detachment that brought with them two Land Rovers equipped with heavy machine guns. I was partial to Land Rovers, having owned one in the past. I liked the look of the sturdy vehicles, bristling with their mounted machine guns, parked in our little compound. As I looked out past the Land Rovers at the miles and miles of dehydrated terrain I found some irony in the fact that our entourage included both U.S. Navy SEALs and Royal Navy personnel. I was happy to have them "on board," all the same.

Over the next couple of days it became apparent that our bombing and probes at the airport were paying off, as we could observe less and less activity there. Karzai was at the same time trying to negotiate a surrender of the Taliban. While we were hopeful that the end was near, we were receiving reports that the Taliban and al-Qa'ida were taking advantage of the negotiations and using the time to secretly flee Kandahar or otherwise melt into the local populace. The only thing we knew for sure about the enemy was that he wasn't stacking arms and turning himself in, so we proceeded accordingly.

In an effort to find out what exactly was the situation in the city of Kandahar, Shirzai sent in a recon party to check it out. Pat, dressed in Afghan garb, accompanied them. In downtown Kandahar, they made it into the

Governor's Palace, which the Taliban and al-Qa'ida had been using as a headquarters, and discovered it was abandoned. Learning this, Shirzai told me that he wanted to move into Kandahar the next day.

Neither Hank nor I could see any tactical reason to delay going in, although in my reading between the lines of Headquarters cables, my sense was that their preference was for Karzai to enter the city first, probably for political reasons. The problem was that Karzai's forces had just taken a major hit with the errant bombing, and it was not clear just how quickly they would be able to move down to Kandahar. It reminded me a bit of the question of who would enter Paris first during War World II, General Patton or Field Marshal Montgomery. I did not see it as a competition between Karzai and Shirzai—and by extension Echo and Foxtrot teams—but I did believe that both forces and their respective teams should try to enter the city as soon as possible. The sooner we were in Kandahar, the sooner we could begin our hunt for al-Qa'ida and related time-sensitive intelligence. To my mind, this trumped any other consideration.

Late that evening as we prepared our gear for the next morning's move, we received intelligence reporting that indicated Taliban leader Mullah Omar planned to escape from Kandahar sometime that night. Headquarters requested that we be on the lookout for a convoy trying to get through our lines. Shirzai sent word out to his fighters to be on the alert, but the night passed without incident.

The next morning, as we loaded our gear into the pickups for our movement into Kandahar, a follow-on request related to Mullah Omar came in. A convoy had been spotted from the air during the night about 20 kilometers from Takhteh-Pol. It was bombed and destroyed, and Foxtrot was tasked to go check it out and see if any of the bodies were that of Mullah Omar. The cable specified that no U.S. military personnel could be involved in the operation. I was not clear why there was a restriction, but I suspected it was due to legal restraints related to the Title 50 and Title 10 authorities. As we did not want to delay our arrival at Kandahar any longer, I asked John to take a security force of Shirzai's fighters and go locate the destroyed convoy to see if Mullah Omar was among the dead, and then join us in Kandahar at the Governor's Palace. We also decided to leave a presence of fighters in Takhteh-Pol in case the situation in Kandahar proved to be untenable and we needed to withdraw.

When the convoy preparations were complete, the pickups and larger trucks pulled into position to begin the road march. This was an important moment for me, one that I had been moving toward in fits and starts ever since I first saw the awful images of the attacks at the World Trade Center. *Had it only been 12 weeks?* It seemed so much longer.

The dual cab of my pickup was full of passengers and equipment so I climbed into the pickup bed. As I did, I noticed that the two burlap sacks of horse feed were in the back of the pickup in front of me. Two heavily armed SEALs who had recently joined us were adjusting them for use as seats during the ride into Kandahar. *Well, at last they are being put to some use*, I thought.

I wore a black stocking cap on my head and sand goggles to protect my eyes from the dust that was sure to come. I sat in the rear corner of the pickup bed with the butt of my AK-47 braced against my lap and the barrel pointed upward. I imagined I looked like a character from a "Mad Max" movie.

The convoy was finally formed and the signal to move out given. This was the moment we had all been waiting for and it was exhilarating; at least that was how I felt. One of Shirzai's fighters was sitting on top of the closed tailgate of a nearby pickup. I didn't think that was such a good idea. When the truck's turn to move came, it lurched forward and the Afghan fell off backward and landed with a dull thud and a puff of dust. The convoy stopped three feet after starting. It was not the dramatic departure I had envisioned. The fighter got back in the truck laughing, no worse for the wear, and we started forward again.

About halfway to the bridge, I saw the two SEALs stand up in the truck bed and toss the bags of horse feed out of the pickup onto the side of the road. The seat idea wasn't working out. The bags looked sad and forlorn laying there on the barren plain as we rolled past, and I contemplated the unlikely journey those two products of Iowa had made.

We reached the bridge and drove across, passing the turn-off to the airport that had already been largely secured by Shirzai's fighters. Continuing on toward Kandahar we began to see the effects of our bombing campaign. Along sections of the highway there were destroyed and burned out vehicles. Bodies twisted and dismembered were littered here and there; their contorted positions suggested the idea of a giant hand having violently flung them onto the ground like rag dolls.

An unnatural stillness lay over the entire scene, a seeming after-effect of the deadly violence that had suddenly visited. Whatever the cause, the stillness was palpable and it commanded my attention as we passed through the area.

Ahead of us I spotted a body that appeared to be sitting upright on a paved portion of the road. A few feet behind it, was the burned out hulk of a large truck, its tires completely melted off. As we drove by, I saw the body had no bottom half, and its upper torso somehow balanced upright. A large stain of what I could only imagine was blood darkened the pavement around it.

Had he been driving the truck when the bombs began to rain down? Did he try to make a run for it? The grotesque image begged these questions and more.

Passing out of the zone of destruction, we began to encounter some buildings along the road. Soon there were more of them, and we knew we had reached the outskirts of Kandahar. We were alert, thinking anything could happen. As we penetrated further into the city, the road narrowed. There were Afghans walking about, but we had yet to see a single vehicle. The pedestrians shot us occasional glances, but nothing more. Their expressionless faces gave nothing away about how they felt about our entrance into their city.

A bit further we started to encounter an occasional car or pickup, and soon a convoy of five or six pickups came down the road toward us from the opposite direction. As the two convoys passed each other, each slowed down due to the narrowness of the street. Like ours, the trucks in the other convoy were full of heavily armed men. We were so close we could have reached out and touched each other. If there was ever a modern opportunity to play Sioux warrior and "count coup," this was it. They looked at us. We looked at them. *Who are these guys? Taliban?* I thought to myself. If anyone had started shooting it would have been a bloody mess. No one did. The episode reminded of a scene from the film "The Longest Day" in which a German and an American patrol pass right by each other neither firing a shot. I remember having thought it was a ridiculous scene that never could have happened.

Passing through a market area, the pedestrian and vehicular traffic became much more congested. A shopkeeper looked up at us and scowled, gesturing at us with a knife. *This native was not friendly.*

Finally we reached the Governor's Palace where Shirzai had once held power before being deposed by the Taliban. High, thick walls surrounded the palace compound that included two main buildings separated by a courtyard with a small decorative water fountain. Shirzai moved into his old building, and Foxtrot team and the ODA moved into the other one.

Shirzai's fighters established a security perimeter around the palace's exterior as we set up our communications gear inside its protective walls. I could now transmit the message I had been waiting to send.

"FOXTROT IN KANDAHAR. ALL PERSONNEL ACCOUNTED FOR."

We were the first team to make it into the city, and I thought it ironic that the date was December 7th, the day the Japanese bombed Pearl Harbor 60 years earlier. For me, December 7th would no longer be a day of infamy, but a day of triumph.

But I also thought about that day in September that had started it all and had set the path that I and the other men around me had taken since. And, as extraordinary as it was that I was now standing in Kandahar some three months later, it seemed right that I was there, and I would not have wanted to be anywhere else.

33

Paying the Freight

John SOON REJOINED US at the Governor's Palace and reported he found the destroyed convoy Mullah Omar was suspected of riding in, but there were no bodies at the site. Local residents had already collected them and brought them into their small village. Mullah Omar was known to be missing an eye he had lost in the war against the Soviets, so with this in mind, John had the grisly chore of checking to see if any of the bodies had this identifying characteristic. It wasn't CSI but it was John's field expedient way to determine that Mullah Omar was in fact not among the dead.

Immediately we began to search the Governor's Palace compound for booby traps and anything of intelligence value. Al-Qa'ida and the Taliban had occupied this place until very recently, and we assumed they had probably left a surprise or two for us. In the courtyard, a young Afghan fighter was digging through a pile of discarded items when there was a muted "pop" and he let out a scream. His thumb was a bloody mess. We suspected he had picked up a detonator cap and somehow set it off, but we really didn't know what had caused the small blast. A medic from the ODA tended to his wound and was able to save the thumb.

Surprisingly, we did not find any other explosive material, hidden or otherwise. We did find numerous boxes of what appeared to be receipts and other miscellaneous forms and papers. Additionally, an Afghan volunteer brought in some boxes of documents he claimed to have taken at gunpoint from an al-Qa'ida member who he caught leaving the rubble of a bombed-out al-Qa'ida safe house. We paid him for his efforts, and Mark secured all the material and began to sort through it on a systematized basis.

Because there was so much of it, Mark performed a triage of sorts with priority going to anything that might be threat-related. The boxes of Taliban receipts were put aside, and he focused on the remaining material. Using an isolated room in the Governor's compound, the material was spread out into different piles on a large Afghan rug. Literally sitting on the floor among the documents, he began the tedious review. This was complicated by the fact that the material was not in English. Despite these challenges it wasn't long before he found something of extreme importance—a plan to carry out an attack in Singapore against the U.S. aircraft carrier *Carl Vinson* and its crew while they were on shore leave. Other targets such as embassies and U.S.-affiliated businesses were identified as well.

The plan was complete with sketches, a video casing, and accompanying surveillance reports. The icing on the cake was a list of cellphone numbers for the members of a Southeast Asia-based al-Qa'ida-affiliated terrorist cell, which was to carry out the attack. Based on this information, Mark drafted up an intelligence report that Foxtrot sent out under immediate precedence. The captured material was considered to be of such importance that within a few days Mark would hand-carry the material to Islamabad for handover to an FBI representative, thus ending Mark's service as a Foxtrot team member on a very high note.

Collecting intelligence that could be used to pre-empt a terrorist attack, particularly one on the scale of the attack planned against the U.S.S. *Carl Vinson*, was the highest goal of an intelligence officer, and it was precisely the reason we were in Kandahar. To my mind, that one intelligence report alone paid Foxtrot's freight to get there.

Another interesting, but much less important, find was a black 4-door armored BMW sedan that belonged to the Taliban's leader, Mullah Omar. Parked under some trees, no doubt to keep it from being seen from the air, it was completely covered in a thick coating of bird shit. The prodigious amount of excrement baffled me as I hadn't seen a single bird since I had entered Afghanistan. I suspected there was a metaphor hidden in this mystery, but I didn't bother to figure it out.

The BMW obviously had not been driven in quite some time, and after it was checked for explosives we tried to get it started, without success. The

Brits saw this as a challenge and continued to try to diagnose the problem but to no avail. The car refused to start.

* *

Although it took some weeks, the intelligence contained in Mark's report would be used to track down and arrest a large al-Qa'ida-affiliated cell in Southeast Asia, thereby neutralizing the threat against the *Carl Vinson* and perhaps other targets as well. According to a 12 January 2002 *Washington Post* article, Singaporean authorities gave credit for the prevention of the attack to intelligence collected in Afghanistan by "coalition forces" in December 2001. This was believed to be the first instance where intelligence collected in Afghanistan was used to prevent a terrorist attack outside the country.

Though we did not know it at the time, also among the captured documents was a filled-in al-Qa'ida membership application form by Jose Padilla, who would be dubbed the "dirty bomber" in press reporting. Mark would one day testify in disguise at Padilla's trial regarding the chain of custody of the application form. The form proved to be a crucial piece of evidence in linking Padilla to al-Qa'ida, and in leading to his conviction on terrorism charges. The successful conviction of Padilla was not an insignificant success in the war on terror, and Foxtrot team's contribution to it represented yet another payment of bills incurred in getting to Kandahar.

34

Link-up with Echo Team

Hamid KARZAI AND ELEMENTS of Echo Team, along with the SF Command and Control Element, arrived in Kandahar on 8 and 9 December, and took up temporary residence at Mullah Omar's compound on the western edge of the city. Shirzai was asked to come to a meeting with Karzai and some local tribal leaders. Foxtrot team was anxious to link up with Echo team, and a few of us accompanied Shirzai to Mullah Omar's compound.

Upon arrival we saw crowds of people walking around, many of them members of the international press that had descended on the town with Karzai's arrival. It was not something we had anticipated or desired. With the exception of a Navy SEAL officer who accompanied us, we wore civilian clothing and were fully armed Westerners. It was impossible to keep a low profile as we walked around trying to find where the meeting was to take place and to locate Echo team. At some point we noticed a crowd headed in the direction of a large building, and the SEAL officer and I merged in with it. As we walked through the walled entranceway, I noticed that international news correspondent Nick Roberts was walking right beside me, a film crew close behind.

Inside was a huge room with a massive Afghan carpet covering the floor and a couple dozen gray-bearded crossed-legged Afghan elders sitting around it. Standing behind them three rows deep were observers, many of them members of the press awaiting Karzai's arrival. I spotted an Afghan I recognized from when I was with Echo team in Jacobabad. I walked over and kneeled down beside him and asked where the Americans were. His English was almost non-existent but even that was better than my Pashto, and he somehow managed to tell me where the team was.

As I stood up to leave, Karzai entered the room from the other side and spotted me. Calling out my name he walked across the center of the room and warmly embraced me.

I was happy to see Karzai again but the moment was anything but inconspicuous, as all eyes in the room were watching him. I told Karzai that we would talk later, and I quickly left to find Echo team. While my encounter with Karzai was taking place, the SEAL officer walked over to Nick Roberts and asked that his film crew not photograph any of the Americans present, a request he complied with.

I found Echo team in a small building in another part of Mullah Omar's compound. They had clearly made themselves at home. As I stepped through the door, a fresh pot of Starbucks was brewing on the coffee maker and the opening notes of the song "Thank You" by Dido filled the air from a portable CD player. I had not heard a female voice in weeks, and as Dido's lyrics began, she slayed me. I stopped in my tracks just to drink in the sensuousness of her voice. It was heavenly - tantalizing, in fact. Until that moment I had never fully appreciated just how sexy a woman's voice could be and her song smote me.

A few of the team members were there, and it was great to see them again. After catching up on our respective situations, I talked to them about what happened with the errant bombing. Don, the deputy team chief for Echo, shared with me that when the bomb hit he was sitting a few feet from a plate glass window typing a report in a building located a short distance from the observation post that had been destroyed. He told me that an instant before the explosion, it felt like a hand had grabbed his shoulder and shoved him forward under the window just before it was blown into the room. He said had he not been thrown forward, the flying glass would have shredded him. It was a strange, inexplicable thing, he said. The bombing had only happened a few days before, and I could see he really didn't know what to make of the event and was still processing it.

The other stories I was told about the bombing confirmed what I had imagined. It had been a nightmare for everyone. But despite the brutal circumstances, they had all pulled together—the CIA officers, the SF soldiers, and a special operations element that was with them at the time—to deal with the catastrophe of the mass casualty event. The closest air medevac capability was part of a Marine Expeditionary Unit designated Task Force 58 located in the south of Helmand province near the Pakistan border. This location was identified as Forward Operating Base-Rhino. The MEU was the only U.S. conventional ground force in Afghanistan, and its mission was to block the escape of enemy fighters trying to cross the border in the area. When the Marines denied the request for an immediate daylight Medevac, Colonel Steve Hadley with the Air Force Special Ops Squadron in Jacobabad had responded with a helicopter air rescue, the first ever undertaken in daylight in Afghanistan. His courageous decision against standing directives prohibiting daylight flights over Afghanistan, and the employment of his medical skills at the scene and during the air extraction, had undoubtedly saved the lives of some of the severely wounded Americans and Afghans. If a Most Valuable Player award were given for support to the U.S. efforts in southern Afghanistan in 2001, Steve Hadley would have my vote hands down.

After spending some time with Echo team, and stopping to listen to Dido one more time, I rejoined Karzai with a couple of other Americans. This time we met in a more private setting in a residence on the compound. Karzai was with several family members whom he introduced to me. They were all very cordial and it was a nice meeting. Karzai was getting ready to fly to an international meeting to formally accept his selection as the head of an interim Afghan government. On the eve of his departure he was relaxed, and as we sipped tea and talked about what was ahead, there was an atmosphere of optimism in the room. I didn't want to take up too much of his time, and when I made my exit, Karzai stepped outside with me for a moment.

In the distance, kites that had been banned by the Taliban and had not been flown for years were fluttering high over the rooftops. Perhaps inspired by the sight of them I told Karzai, "I think God is smiling on Afghanistan today."

"Yes," he said. "I think so as well."

35

Raids, Rubble, Rocks, and Lingerie

Within A COUPLE OF days, Echo team had moved to another compound on the opposite side of the city from Mullah Omar's, and the SF Command and Control Element joined us at the Governor's Palace. A couple more SF A teams also arrived and set up with us as well. With the addition of the new personnel, the American presence in the compound swelled to around 75 people.

One of the first orders of business was to arrange the handover of Kandahar Airport from Shirzai's fighters to the Marines moving up from Forward Operating Base-Rhino in southern Helmand province. The goal was to do this while drawing as little attention as possible to the fact that U.S. Marines were in the Kandahar area. To achieve this, an SF element met the Marines in the middle of the night and escorted them around the outskirts of Kandahar to the airport where the handover took place. Just so the Marines did not forget who was there first, the ODA had already painted its radio call sign "Texas 17" high up on the airport's water tower.

Within a day or two I traveled out to the airport to meet up with Charlie, the CIA liaison officer attached to the Marine Expeditionary Unit. Charlie was a friend of mine whom I had known since my first days at the Agency, and as a former Marine, he was one of the paramilitary instructors when I went through some of my early training. Charlie had been in Islamabad when I had passed through there before joining Echo team. He was looking to get on a team going to Afghanistan and had jumped at the chance to join up with the Marines.

It was good to see him there in the Afghan desert. He seemed in good spirits, although he told me the last few weeks had been frustrating for him and the Marines. According to Charlie, while at Rhino Base in Helmand Province, the MEU had been kept on a pretty tight leash and had been limited to mostly defensive operations. Staying on the defense was not part of the Marines make-up, but as the only conventional U.S force in the country, it was what was required to keep the American military profile low.

Charlie walked me around parts of the airfield and pointed out where the Marines had constructed some basic POW holding facilities made of concertina wire. For the moment the cages were empty, at least the ones I saw, but the hope was that surrendering Taliban and al-Qa'ida would soon be filling them up.

Our next stop was to meet the MEU commander, a one-star general named James Mattis, about whom Charlie had nothing but praise. Mattis invited us into his office. A big coffee cup already in his hand, he had an orderly bring us some as well. Down to earth and unassuming, he provided us with a short, informal briefing about the MEU and the situation at the airport. Myself and another member of Foxtrot team who had accompanied me reciprocated, explaining who we were and our current understanding of the situation in Kandahar. The entire meeting lasted no more than 15 minutes.

After the meeting, as we were walking out to our pickups, Charlie asked me for a favor. He had no long gun and was armed only with his Glock-19. He asked if I could get him an Agency rifle. He said the Marines had at times loaned him an M-4, but he needed his own rifle. I knew Echo team had been supplied with M-4's at some point and I told him I would pass the request on to them, which I did. I never saw Charlie in Afghanistan again and I don't know if he ever got his rifle.

Another priority task was to carry out raids against locations in Kandahar that CIA Headquarters believed were al-Qa'ida safe houses. We suspected they would have been abandoned, but we really didn't know for sure until we checked. Regardless, we were hopeful that we could still find materials of intelligence value.

Even prior to arriving in Kandahar, Foxtrot team had been working with Shirzai to create a special counterterrorism unit of 50 better-than-average fighters for carrying out these raids. The night before we were to begin the raids, Khalil came to me and complained that the recently arrived Army lieutenant colonel in charge of the SF CCE had told him that the Afghan counterterrorism unit was now under the colonel's command. This was news to me. I found the colonel and explained that we had been putting this force together for some time for the express purpose of carrying out the safe house raids when we reached Kandahar, and that if he needed fighters, Shirzai had plenty of others from which to choose. The colonel responded that, no, he wanted this group as they were better trained. He went on to say that, as the senior U.S. military commander on the ground, he was in charge of all allied armed forces, and therefore the CT unit was under his command.

On the surface, the colonel seemed to have a valid point. Unquestionably he was the senior U.S. military officer, and depending on the terms of joint-agreements made with the Afghans, his rank could put him in charge of allied forces. It was a concept with which I was familiar. The colonel's rationale was specious, however, as Shirzai's forces were not, in fact, "allied forces." Shirzai had not signed any alliance agreement with the U.S. military. Rather, he and his forces were operating as counterterrorism assets, managed and supported by the CIA as authorized under Title 50, the legal authority under which the war was being fought at the time. The truth was, both as a practical and legal matter, it was only through the CIA's auspices that the SF ODA's were working with Shirzai's fighters, and that work was in an advise and support role, not a command role.

Still, I had no interest in getting into a legal debate or turf battle over who controlled Shirzai's forces. In the interest of maintaining a good relationship I held my fire, avoiding what I believed would have been a contentious, unproductive, and ultimately, destructive debate. I was glad I did so. The next day an understanding was reached that CIA officers and ODA members would conduct joint raids supported by the special Afghan CT unit.

As we suspected, all the houses we raided were abandoned by al-Qa'ida, but we did find some material of interest at some of the targeted locations. In one house there were a lot of newspapers, magazines, and other printed material. Keeping an eye out for booby-traps, I rummaged through it and came upon an English language technical magazine. On the cover it highlighted an article that rated the best flight training simulators on the market. In the same house we found the carton in which a flight simulator had been packaged. As I examined the carton, images of the hijacked aircraft crashing into the World Trade Center Towers flashed through my mind. *Had the terrorists used this flight simulator as part of their preparation for their mission on 9/11? Was this the house where they once stayed?* Odds were the answer was yes.

On another day, some of us traveled out to Tarnak Farms south of Kandahar, where al-Qa'ida had maintained its premier training facility. It had been one of the first targets of the bombing campaign. All that remained of the place was rubble. We spent a few hours poking around the shattered remnants of the buildings looking for anything of intelligence value.

During this search we discovered a small underground room broken open by bombs and fully exposed to daylight. In the room were numerous metal footlockers filled with dark blue semi-precious Lapis Lazuli stones which al-Qa'ida used for trading purposes. Before loading them up for transport back to Kandahar, we each stuck one of the blue uncut rocks in our pocket. The souvenir-taking reminded me of the scene in the book "Slaughterhouse-Five" when the character Rosewater, commenting on Billy Pilgrim's wedding diamond taken as war booty, says, "That is the attractive thing about war. Everybody gets a little something."

There were other attractive things, too. Pieces of women's lingerie were found scattered around in the rubble. I could not say what brand it was, but it was as sexy as the Victoria Secrets line, and it gave rise to jokes about what kind of training had been going on at Tarnak Farms.

That evening after my return to the Governor's Palace I was invited to watch a movie being shown by one of Hank's ODA members. I had not seen a movie since I had left home and readily accepted the invitation. The film was a relatively recent fictional drama about a high-altitude climbing expedition. It was shown on a computer in a little room with some of the ODA members crowded in close to the small screen. I found a seat on the floor and was quickly caught up in the story. Although a drama with moments of life and death tension, I felt relaxed and comforted in watching it, and in being entertained and completely absorbed by something different than the life I had been living.

After the movie ended, I realized just how much of a mental escape it had been for me. I also realized that I felt guilty about it. Somehow my forgetting about where I was and what I was doing just felt wrong to me. It almost felt like it was a risky thing for me to have done—that I needed to stay fully engaged in the reality I was living and not allow myself any escape from that reality until it was time for me to leave Afghanistan.

36

Tensions Among the Tribe

With THE FALL OF Kandahar, and Karzai's emergence as the leader of the transitional government to come, simmering frictions between Shirzai and Karzai came to a head. A major catalyst for this was Karzai's decision to appoint Mullah Naqib Alikhozai, the former Taliban governor of Kandahar, as the new head of security for the province. This decision enraged Shirzai. Even before we had entered Kandahar, Shirzai's informants were reporting that Naqib was involved in helping al-Qa'ida fighters escape from the city. This was taking place even as Naqib was supposedly negotiating with Karzai the surrender of Kandahar. Shirzai would have no part of the new plan, and he threatened to challenge Karzai's authority to appoint Naqib without his consent as the governor of Kandahar.

The growing rift between the two Pashtun leaders set off alarm bells in Washington, as it could have resulted in the splintering of the fragile, but much needed united anti-Taliban Pashtun front. To head the situation off before it became any worse, Greg and I were directed by Headquarters to meet with the two men to see if we could get them to come to a meeting of the minds on the Mullah Naqib issue.

When the meeting took place I asked Mark to come along. Throughout our time on the ground in Afghanistan, I considered him to be Foxtrot's

"Shirzai expert," and when it came to anything of consequence involving Shirzai I wanted him to be in a position to weigh in on the issue. An ardent supporter of Shirzai, over the last several weeks Mark had grown to believe that he was not getting the credit he was due for his accomplishments in the south, and that Karzai was being favored. I actually agreed with him, but I did not take it as personally as Mark seemed to, or believe it was a deliberate decision being taken by Headquarters to disenfranchise Shirzai. To my mind the apparent favoritism was rather a natural result of Headquarters' recognition that if he survived, Karzai, not Shirzai, would likely become the leader of Afghanistan. On this point, when there was something in the cable traffic that seemed to support Mark's belief, and I did not seem to be affected by it, Mark would shake his head and say, "Man, you have the patience of Job."

At the meeting, Greg took the lead, and he did not beat around the bush in laying out Washington's concerns to the two tribal leaders. Shirzai was not cowed, however, and in the ensuing discussions made his case that Mullah Naqib was a snake and could never be trusted. In the end, Karzai agreed to look into Shirzai's charges. Mark did not say a word throughout the meeting. I knew that he was furious that Karzai was even considering the appointment of Naqib to a government position, and I think it was everything he could do to keep his anger from showing.

Within a day or two, Karzai through his own sources confirmed Shirzai's derogatory information about Naqib, and he agreed that Naqib would not have any position in the new government. An inter-Pashtun crisis was avoided, to Washington's relief.

37

Death from Above

"Never turn away free man or slave, by day or night, though you may be sleeping, eating, or bathing, if he says he has news for you."

Nicephorus II Phocas
Byzantine Emperor

It WAS THE MORNING of December 16th, the day of the Muslim holiday of Eid al-Fitr that marks the end of Ramadan, and I was brushing my teeth at an outdoor wash station in the courtyard of the Governor's Palace. Khalil approached and reported to me that an Afghan had walked up to the perimeter security and had asked to speak with an American.

I put away my toothbrush and told Khalil to have the man searched and then brought to me. In a few minutes, I met the man, whose name was Moktar. Through Khalil he told me that he had tried to come into the compound the previous day, but the Afghan guards had turned him away. He had decided he must try again, however. He pointed to the building occupied by Shirzai and his staff no more than 50 feet away and said there were many explosives buried in the dirt roof of the building. He claimed that they would be detonated that night during the Eid al-Fitr breaking of the fast banquet. Moktar seemed confident in what he was saying, and I saw little to be gained by him making up the story and coming to tell us.

Fortunately, we were in an excellent position to check out Moktar's tale, which is often not the case with a walk-in who volunteers information. Only a few hours earlier a team of bomb technicians from the CIA's Office of Technical Services, or OTS, had arrived to support our operations in the Kandahar area. They brought with them hundreds of pounds of technical gear, so if anyone could figure out if there were explosives in the roof, they could.

I had Khalil wait with Moktar while I found the OTS team chief. He was cocooned in a sleeping bag completely zonked out among his teammates, all similarly cocooned and zonked. The poor guy had only been asleep for two or three hours after a grueling marathon trip from the States, so I felt bad about having to roust him from his sleep.

"Hey, Mike. Wake up, man. Sorry, but I've got to put you to work."

Mike slowly opened his bloodshot eyes which had that look of *where the hell am I and who the hell are you?* in them. He then stiffly sat up, and I let him have a few more seconds to get his wits about him. I then gave him the Cliff Notes brief on Moktar. With the mention of explosives, Mike was fully awake and firing on all cylinders.

I took him to meet Moktar, and while Mike talked to him I went into Shirzai's building. In anticipation of the night's festivities, his staff was already arranging the place settings around the edges of a large Afghan carpet that covered the floor of the banquet room that was directly beneath the suspect roof. I found Shirzai in his office, and through one of his English-speaking staff I told him about the reported explosives. I insisted that he and his staff leave the building immediately until the threat could be evaluated. He reluctantly agreed, and everyone in the building moved outside and away from the building.

It didn't take Mike and his team long to determine that Moktar's information was accurate. The roof was filled with buried Russian land mines and 122mm artillery rockets rigged with detonators for command detonation. For me, it was lightning and snakes all over again, although worse because they were only feet away, coiled and nested together, and ready to strike.

As relayed by Moktar, some weeks earlier the Taliban and al-Qa'ida had anticipated that if they had to flee Kandahar before Ramadan ended, either Shirzai or Karzai would likely establish himself at the Governor's Palace and that he would host a breaking of the fast celebration on Eid al-Fitr. Present would be his commanders, important tribal leaders, and his American friends—all the ingredients for a juicy, or in this case, bloody, target.

It was a prescient and shrewd plan. The Taliban was now poised to wipe out half of their armed opposition's leadership in the south with the push of a button. The detonation of the buried explosives would also do massive damage to the co-located U.S. military and intelligence presence in the south, dealing the U.S. effort in Afghanistan a huge blow and setting back much of what had been gained.

Using its sophisticated gear, the OTS team located the command detonation cord that ran off the compound, and neutralized it with a small cutting charge. The explosives could no longer be detonated remotely. While the immediate threat was gone, there was so much ordnance packed into the roof—2,500 lbs. of it to be precise—it would require many days to safely remove it.

The reality of how close we had come to catastrophe was sobering. All it would have taken for that disaster to happen would have been for Moktar not to have returned back to the Governor's compound a second time after having been turned away on his first attempt to warn us. With this in mind, I met with him a final time, both to thank him and to pay him. The first part was easy. The second part was a bit more complicated. I was flush with cash at that point, as the OTS team had just brought me a replenishment of a million dollars. So funds were available and the man had undoubtedly just saved dozens of lives, quite possibly mine included. *So how much was that worth?* The word "priceless" came to mind, although it was a bit hard for me to be objective about the matter.

Someone on Foxtrot suggested a payment to Moktar of $300, rationalizing that $300 is a lot of money in Afghanistan for a man of Moktar's economic status, and it should make him happy. If we gave him more, the reasoning continued, his sudden affluence could bring suspicion on him from Taliban still in the area and result in bad things happening to him and his family.

Having once lost an agent for this very reason, I was sympathetic to the argument. *But $300!* No way, we had to do better than that. Finally, I gave Moktar $2,500. It was a princely sum for him, but a paltry sum for us considering what we had gotten, or perhaps more importantly, had not gotten, out of the deal. Was it the right amount? I didn't know. There aren't any books that tell you these kinds of things, but that is what I gave him.

Remembering the agent I had once lost, I also gave him a warning that if anyone found out he had the money he would likely be killed, either by a thief or by his erstwhile friends, the Taliban, who would assume he was an American agent. Either way, I told him, "You will be dead."

38

Do I Go or Do I Stay

The NEXT DAY I learned that the schedule for my return to the States had been moved up. I was to catch a ride back to Jacobabad on a MC-130 that would be at the Kandahar airport that very night. Although I knew my departure date was approaching, now that it was unexpectedly upon me I had conflicting feelings about leaving, and I considered whether I should go.

On the one hand, the timing seemed right. Our mission to capture Kandahar had been accomplished. Al-Qa'ida in Afghanistan had been smashed, and what was left of it was badly wounded and on the run. My team no longer existed, as Foxtrot and Echo had been unceremoniously combined under Greg's command a couple of days before.

On the other hand, I knew that there was still work to be done, and that the Afghanistan story was far from over. I also had to admit to myself that I actually liked being in Afghanistan, that I felt more fully alive in a way that I had not felt before, and that without a doubt I was living the greatest adventure of my life.

In part, this was due to the element of danger that had always been present, but in equal part it was because of the freedom my teammates and I had experienced in dealing with the uncertainties and challenges we faced. This had meant that whatever decisions we made, we did so knowing our fate and our mission's success was in our own hands and no one else's. To its credit, Headquarters had recognized the dynamic nature of the Afghanistan theater of operations and had refrained from dictating actions from thousands of miles away, allowing the teams on the ground to operate in a near autonomous fashion and to call the shots as each saw fit. This approach was a blessing to every CIA officer who was serving in Afghanistan at the time.

Yet another reason why I had come to like being in Afghanistan had not so much to do with mission, or even having the freedom to make my own decisions, but rather it had to do with the environment in which I was living. It was simply more satisfying to spend my days outside, surrounded by stunningly stark vistas and drenched by the clear sunlight of the high desert than it was to pass so much of my time sitting in a fluorescent-lit building staring into a computer screen. Life in Afghanistan had a course texture to it compared to the smooth plastic feel of life in America, or for that matter, most other modern countries. I knew I would miss that coarseness and the authenticity it seemed to give to each day. This realization made me consider the not insignificant price that I was paying to be a member of our modern civilization, and its ramifications went far beyond whether I should stay in Afghanistan or not.

But of a more immediate nature, when I thought about my brief Afghanistan sojourn, the truth was that despite its horribly tragic catalyst and ongoing hardships and dangers, my experiences beginning on the day after 9/11 to that moment had taken place during what seemed to be an otherworldly time, almost as if a parenthesis had been inserted into the cosmic flow, within which normal procedures and conventions did not apply. Individuals and organizations had sacrificed and cooperated toward a common cause at a level I had never before witnessed. At a personal level, people just treated each other better than they had previously. Turf and ego battles, with the rarest of exceptions, had not surfaced, at least not at the level at which I was operating, and the focus had been only on the mission. Unquestionably, it had been an extraordinary time, during which I had worked with extraordinary people who had put aside any fear they had, and with great courage they had done a job that had to be done. My feelings about leaving Afghanistan reminded me of General Lee's observation to Longstreet at Fredericksburg when he is reported to have said, "It is well that war is so terrible, lest we grow too fond of it." The General definitely knew what he was talking about.

But I also knew that all good things had to come to an end, as would this unique period of unfettered cooperation and respectful interaction. The handwriting was already on the wall, as plans were being made for introducing large numbers of conventional U.S. military forces into the country, even as CIA worked to bolster its own presence many times over. What we had would not last under these circumstances, and the cosmic parentheses would soon disappear. Too many bureaucratic interests apart from mission, and too many over-sized egos that infected all large institutions would ensure that.

I had been privileged and fortunate to serve at this special time, and the thought came to me that maybe I should "get while the getting is good." The other thought that arose was the promise that I had made to my wife, in what seemed like eons ago, that I would come home as soon as I could. Well, "as soon as I could" meant getting on that MC-130 that night. With that thought in mind I made my decision.

Unfortunately, Shirzai had left that morning for a visit to another part of the province so I could not say goodbye to him. I felt badly about this. What he and his fighters had done for the U.S. was hard to overstate. By acting as surrogate ground forces against our enemies, many American lives and much treasure had been saved. I wanted to personally thank him for this, but it would have to remain unfinished business.

39

Jacobabad Revisited

I ARRIVED BACK IN Jacobabad early in the morning. I had more gear than I wanted to carry, so I hiked over to the CIA tent to get a pickup to transport it. I woke up Doug and asked him for the truck keys. He started to get up but I told him there was no need and to stay in bed. He asked me if I was sure I didn't need his help, and I said no thanks, I'm fine. He went back to bed and I drove over and picked up the gear, and then racked out at the tent until daylight came.

Later I was told that Doug saw my consideration to let him sleep as evidence that my time in Afghanistan had "changed" me for the better, and that I was no longer the jerk he had encountered when he had tried to get me to sign for the money.

In the morning I learned there was another CIA team at Jacobabad that had been waiting to go into Afghanistan, but it had been ordered to return to Islamabad to await a later deployment. The CIA team leader and an SF Sergeant named Nathan Chapman, as well as myself, headed over to the Air Force mess hall for breakfast. Over my first American-style breakfast in many weeks, we talked about the situation in Afghanistan, with the team leader expressing concern that it would all be over before his team even got there. I told him not to worry. It wasn't going to be over for a while. It was a relaxing hour, and as we all do, Nathan talked about his wife and kids back home. At some point, one of them asked me when I would leave for the U.S. I glanced down at the date on my watch to figure that out, and when I did I realized for the first time that it was my birthday. The two of them laughed and wished me a happy birthday. For that and other reasons, it was a memorable birthday breakfast.

Afterward I turned my Glock and AK-47 over to Doug. He didn't know that the AK was not the same one I had been issued, and he accepted it without question. Months later, however, my trading out the rifle caught up to me and I was notified that I was the subject of a "Report of Survey" investigation in that there was no record of my having turned in the rifle I was issued. I had to explain why that was the case, and in the end no action was taken against me. It was a small price to pay in order to carry a rifle I felt comfortable with.

I spent the rest of the day in Jacobabad helping the CIA team load its gear onto a C-130 for transport to Islamabad. A few others who were headed up to Islamabad helped out as well, and Nathan and his non-stop jokes and funny stories kept us all laughing. His extroverted personality and quick wit combined to make him a force of nature, and he made a big impression on me.

Late in the afternoon we flew to Islamabad. I only spent a couple of days there. Prior to leaving I looked up the CIA team leader and Nathan to say goodbye. I told both of them that if they made it to Afghanistan to be careful and then repeated what I had once told the Headquarters officer who advised me of Mike Spann's death: Afghanistan is still a dangerous, uncontrolled place, and anything could happen there at any time.

40

Home

I RETURNED TO THE U.S. a couple of days before Christmas, when the holiday season was in full swing. It was wonderful to see the family again, and to drive through our neighborhood and say hello to friends and neighbors who had no idea where I had been. As usual, our house was warmly decorated and the Christmas tree was up and glowing brightly.

Despite the ambiance, I was unable to muster any holiday spirit, and I had the sense that I had left something undone back in Afghanistan; that maybe I had made the wrong decision in coming home. I was taking a few days of leave during the holidays, but I was anxious to get back to work even though I didn't know exactly what that would be when I returned. I did know I'd be reporting back to NE Division and that my time with CTC/SO was at its end.

A couple of weeks later, on my first day back at Headquarters, I decided that before reporting in to my new office I would stop by CTC to say hello to my colleagues there. Because the office had moved, I had to find it, and when I did I was impressed by the large office space it now occupied. The place was completely changed. There were many more people assigned there so a lot of faces I didn't recognize.

While making my cubicle rounds saying hello to the people I knew, I happened to look up at a TV that was tuned to a news channel. I immediately recognized the face in the photograph being shown on the news report, and my stomach knotted up. It was Nathan Chapman, killed in action in Afghanistan. I didn't want to believe it. Memories of the brief time I had spent with him instantly came flooding to my mind. Recalling his unrelenting humor, his irrepressible energy, and generally larger than life personality, made it even harder to accept that he was now dead.

As the news report continued, pictures of his wife and children were shown. They looked like a perfect family, and I remembered Nathan talking about them while we had breakfast together on my birthday only three weeks before. The reporter commented that Nathan was the first soldier to be killed by hostile fire in Afghanistan. Mike Spann was the Agency's first enemy-killed casualty, and now Nathan held that distinction for the military.

The people around me headed off to a staff meeting. I was invited to attend but didn't. After hearing the news of Nathan's death, I just wanted to escape for a while.

I made my way through the rows of now empty cubicles toward the front door. As I did, I passed by a huge video monitor mounted on the wall. On the screen was a video feed that was streaming live images of six ghostly figures slowly making their way in single file down a dark and barren mountainside. They didn't look like much more than stick men, their silhouettes glowing white against the mud-brown color of the ground. It was night where they were and they probably thought they couldn't be seen. But they were wrong. The darkness could not hide them. They were absolutely luminous, in fact.

I looked around to ask if anyone knew where this was taking place, but there was no one to ask. They had all gone to the meeting. It was just the wide screen monitor, the six figures, and me.

There was no sound accompanying the video feed and no noise from the empty office. It was totally quiet. Although the men were thousands of miles away, I felt like I was there, high above their heads, secretly sharing a private moment with them from my omnipotent perch. I continued to watch and noticed that the group was using good military discipline, keeping their distance from one another as they picked their way around rocks and boulders. They made progress, but it was slow and the mountain was big.

Suddenly, silently, something new appeared on the upper left of the screen. It was a piece of earth erupting upward. Circular in shape, it lifted straight out of the ground and directly toward me. It reminded me of a splash of chocolate milk. It was not particularly close to the stick figures, but then, other splashes of earth followed. Rapidly the splashes rose up and within a few seconds they completely filled the screen.

How many splashes were there? I couldn't tell. Dozens I suspected. I knew they had to be caused by bombs from conventional aircraft. The residue from the explosions filled the air and blended into a solid gray haze that obscured my view of what laid below. It didn't matter. I knew that even if I could have seen the ground clearly, I wouldn't have been able to see the stick figures anymore. They had been transformed from ghostly silhouettes to just ghosts.

I realized this was how it had all started those months before. Me standing in front of a screen, not at CIA, but at FBI Headquarters, watching violent images of planes crashing, buildings falling, and people dying. Now it was ending for me in much the same way. The difference this time was that the violence I was watching was not happening in my country, and it was not innocent people who were dying. Given the nature of the counterterrorism business, that was probably as good an indicator of success, or at least progress, as any.

I remained alone standing in front of the now dark monitor in the quiet room. Everyone was still at the meeting. It was business as usual, something I would have to get used to. It was Headquarters after all.

Epilogue

In JANUARY 2002, WHEN I walked out of the Counterterrorist Center and returned to work in the Near East Division, I believed my involvement with Afghanistan was finished. The Agency, however, had other thoughts on the subject, and I was asked to head up the Headquarters office that would support the new CIA station there. It was not an assignment that I had expected. I had assumed I would finally take the liaison officer position I was supposed to have taken months before at the FBI. Fresh from my experience in Afghanistan, however, I felt I had a personal investment in the future of that country, and I agreed to the proposed job. It would prove to be an interesting, although at times frustrating, experience.

During that two-year assignment, I would witness the limited expeditionary nature of the Agency's involvement in Afghanistan transition to that of a large-scale entrenched presence. I would also watch relationships with the military and other government departments become encumbered by the return of bureaucratic practices and self-interested policies that had been minimized immediately after the 9/11 attacks.

Prior to assuming my new position, there had been no CIA station in the country for many years, and so no corresponding Headquarters office existed to support it. Therefore my first task would be to establish what would become the Afghanistan office. It was a "from the ground up" effort, with everything from office space to personnel needing to be found. Fortunately, this initiative was considered a priority by NE Division senior management, and within a relatively short time the new office was up and running. This was fortunate because events in Afghanistan were moving quickly. The fledgling Karzai government was struggling to establish itself, and the U.S. presence in the country was increasing dramatically from the few hundred Americans that were there when I left in December 2001. Had someone at the time told me that the number of Americans in country would one day reach into the many tens of thousands, and that the CIA station there would become the largest in the world, I would not have believed them.

The standup of the Afghanistan desk in NE Division did not mean that my old office in CTC went away. CTC/SO would continue to oversee CIA's counterterrorism effort in Afghanistan, while the Afghanistan office would support the station's traditional intelligence collection operations and liaison activities. To avoid confusion and duplication of effort, a clear definition of roles and responsibilities was required, as well as timely communication between the two offices. Toward that end I regularly attended CTC/SO staff meetings to ensure NE Division was kept in the loop on any significant CT developments in country that could affect NE Division's operations.

Throughout the first half of 2002, many of the assignments of CIA personnel to Afghanistan were for short periods of time, usually averaging three months. This system required a constant rotation of officers, and it very quickly proved to be unsustainable from a personnel management standpoint. It also created problems with the continuity of operations in the field. Compounding these problems was that CIA's mission continued to expand as the U.S. diplomatic presence and the number of U.S. military forces grew. This meant, among other things, that Station needed more resources to recruit and handle agents who could report intelligence on threats against the U.S. presence. As an organization, al-Qa'ida in Afghanistan had been largely destroyed and driven from the country, but serious threats from remaining Taliban elements and the terrorist group known as the Haqqani Network still remained.

As American lives were on the line, the mission to collect intelligence on these groups had to have the highest priority, but it did come at a cost to intelligence reporting on other high priority areas such as political stability in the country. "Mission creep" had arrived, and it became clear that we could not continue to staff and effectively operate our station and bases using mostly short-term officers. To address this, more and more longer-term positions were created, usually for a tour of one year. As these jobs came on line and were filled, the chaotic churn of people rotating in and out of Afghanistan slowed to a more manageable level. That said, the truth remained that CIA was not the U.S. military, and it simply did not have reserves of thousands of personnel that could be drawn upon to meet the ever-expanding intelligence requirements generated by U.S. policymakers and other institutions who needed CIA intelligence to help them do their jobs.

As the months went by, more and more officers were being posted to Afghanistan to serve in locations throughout the country. Of this group, a fair number were volunteers who were actively seeking to be assigned there. On those occasions when a volunteer would stop by my office to discuss a possible assignment in country, I would always try to get a feel for the officer's motivation for wanting to go to Afghanistan. When the motivation seemed principally to be the extra money they would earn as a result of receiving danger pay and other hardship benefits, I would caution him or her that while Afghanistan was more stable than it had been when I was there, it continued to be a dangerous place, and the possibility that they could lose their lives there was a real one. I would ask if they were willing to risk having to pay that price for a bigger paycheck. Some of them were.

While most people's reasons for wanting to serve in Afghanistan were a combination of factors, money being only one, I always believed the most important reason had to be belief in the mission of preventing Afghanistan from ever again becoming a sanctuary from which a terrorist group could strike the U.S. To my way of thinking, belief in this mission was the only thing that could justify putting your life at risk, and it was the only thing that would carry you through the day when circumstances became dangerous and uncertain. It would also be the only thing that would give some comfort to friends and family left behind if tragedy struck.

As I watched from Headquarters while our station and the official U.S. presence in Afghanistan grew, and as I read the intelligence reporting about the security situation there, I knew I needed to go back and see it for myself to really understand how things on the ground had changed since I left. In mid-fall 2002 I packed up my rucksack again, and along with another senior officer named Mike from CTC/SO I traveled back to Afghanistan for a short trip.

*   *   *

In Kabul we met with the Chief of Station and other CIA officers who were working day and night to manage multiple high-priority programs. In most cases these programs were adequately funded so money was not a problem, but insufficient or mismatched staffing was. While there was adequate support and administrative staff, non-managerial level operations officers who ran agents to collect intelligence or worked with the budding Afghan intelligence service made up only a relatively small percentage of the station, and they were stretched thin. In the months ahead, particularly in the lead up to, and after, the invasion of Iraq, having the right number and mix of officers in Afghanistan would continue to be a challenge as priority went to staffing the Iraq effort.

Our second stop was Kandahar, and I was looking forward to returning there. One reason was to see how it had changed, but equally important was that I would see my former Afghan comrade in arms, Gul Agha Shirzai. He was still the governor of Kandahar province, and I wanted to at last personally thank him for his key role in driving al-Qa'ida and the Taliban out of the city.

We arrived at the U.S. military-controlled Kandahar airport on a small agency aircraft. As we approached for landing I looked out to the southeast across the monotone desert landscape to try and spot the village of Takhteh-Pol that had served as Foxtrot team's base during the siege of the airport. My effort was in vain and I felt a sense of disappointment not to be able to see it again. The feeling surprised me and I realized then that the dusty outpost and the events that had transpired there had carved out a special place in my heart and memory.

Once we were on the ground, it was a surreal experience to stand on the tarmac seeing the familiar surrounding terrain, knowing that less than a year earlier the airport had been in the hands of al-Qa'ida, and U.S. bombs called in by Hank and ODA-583 were falling on a near continuous basis in and around the facility. Although those events had not occurred that long ago, the differences in circumstances from then and now made it seem as if it had happened in another lifetime.

On the second evening after our arrival, Mike and I dined with Shirzai at his residence. The venue was a far cry from the parachute-shrouded mud structure I had dined in on that that first night in the Shin Naray Valley back in November 2001. Shirzai looked more fit than I remembered him, but the appearance may just have been the effect of his having clean clothes and a more neatly trimmed beard and hair from when I last saw him. He seemed very much at ease, and from all indications he was comfortable in his role as governor, this despite his having narrowly survived an assassination attempt a few months before.

Shirzai had kept the guest list small with only one or two other Afghans present. Through an interpreter we reminisced about the campaign to capture

Kandahar and how things had changed since then. Noting the Glock pistols Mike and I were carrying, Shirzai commented that he hoped the next time we came to Kandahar we would not need to come armed. As the dinner came to a close, Shirzai said that because I had left Afghanistan before he could say goodbye he had never been able to properly thank me. I told him it was myself and the rest of the American people who owed him and his men the thanks, explaining that if it had not been for them al-Qa'ida might still be occupying southern Afghanistan—either that or a lot of American soldiers would have been put at risk to do the same job his fighters had done. After saying our goodbyes and giving each other a farewell embrace, Shirzai gave a short command to a houseboy who quickly rolled up two Afghan carpets that were on the hallway floor. Shirzai took them and presented them to us, saying, "No one comes to Afghanistan and leaves without a carpet." The carpets were nothing fancy, just simple tribal kilims, and used ones at that, but it was a gift I have always treasured.

*   *   *

We returned to Kabul but had one final destination remaining on our itinerary before returning to the U.S. The town of Asadabad, located in the northeastern part of the country in the province of Nuristan, adjacent to the Pakistan border, was at least as dangerous as Kandahar—perhaps more so, and CIA maintained a small base in the area. One evening after drawing M-4 rifles and armored vests, Mike and I traveled by armored suburban to Kabul airport, and along with some other Agency officers boarded an Mi–8 helicopter. It was the first time I had ever flown in a Russian-made aircraft, and I was a bit apprehensive; however, as it turned out, I liked the helicopter. Instead of lifting off directly into the air, it trundled down the runway on a triad of little, fat tires and then after gaining some speed gently lifted off. Prior to reaching Asadabad we landed at another location, and the officers who had boarded with us got off the aircraft. We took on some fuel, and as rain began to fall we lifted off again and continued on to a small landing strip near the base.

The base was co-located with a sizeable U.S. military force consisting of Army Rangers, Special Forces soldiers, and soldiers of the 82nd Airborne. The CIA contingent was small, however, with only four or five officers assigned. At our orientation briefing, I was impressed with the progress the officers had made in learning about and documenting the Pashtun tribal presence in the region, including details about the key personalities—basic but important information not previously known. Most of the knowledge gained had come from direct interaction with the local population during trips throughout the area that were taken at great risk given that Taliban insurgents were active there.

Another topic of the briefing concerned an operation planned for the very next morning. Its goal was to capture four suspected al-Qa'ida members who, according to base sources, were hiding in a village about 30 kilometers away, up the Pech River Valley. The base had been trying to launch the operation for almost two weeks with the participation of elements of the co-located U.S. military forces. Much to the base's frustration, however, and despite repeated attempts by their military partners, the military headquarters in Kabul would not approve their operations plan. Apparently the problem lay in the air support annex to the plan, which their headquarters found wanting. Proposed refinements had gone back and forth between the military unit and its headquarters, but still the annex was deemed "unsat" and permission for the military units to be involved in the capture operation continued to be denied.

Fearing that the suspected al-Qa'ida members might cross the border into Pakistan in the next few days, the base had reluctantly decided to undertake the operation without the participation of the U.S. military and instead would use a local Afghan force that was trained and supervised by the CIA officers.

The next morning, hours before the sun came up, the raid force, consisting of 12 Afghans, 3 base officers, and me, formed up in a column of 4-wheel drive pickup trucks. Despite my protests that I was just a "rear area headquarters guy," I was assigned the "place of honor" in the convoy—the front passenger seat of the lead pickup. The truck was driven by a hard-as-nails looking Afghan who was the team leader for the Afghan contingent. I was told he was a highly experienced fighter who over the years had been shot on multiple occasions during various gun battles. The knowledge that, in addition to being in the lead vehicle, I was sitting next to a bullet magnet was not reassuring.

In the early morning darkness we pulled out of the base perimeter and made our way to a dirt road that ran along the Pech River, now swollen from the heavy rain that fell the night before. As the base receded in the distance the fact that we were undertaking this mission alone, leaving behind some of the most elite soldiers in the U.S. Army, simply because of bureaucratic difficulties in getting an operations plan approved, did not sit well with me or the other officers. The situation exemplified on a small scale what was happening in Afghanistan as the U.S. military and civilian presence grew, and along with it the bureaucracy and process. Initiative, responsiveness, and flexibility were correspondingly reduced, and mission effectiveness suffered. This would not have happened in 2001.

Our movement along the river was slow due to the generally poor condition of the road. Occasionally we would come to a roadblock guarded by Afghan militias. After a brief chat with the Afghan team leader, the guards would wave us through while eying us curiously as we passed. After a few hours of driving we came to the village where we were to ford the river. By this point the sun had risen above the steep mountains that lined each side of the valley, but there was still a sharp chill in the air as we dismounted the vehicles. The Afghans, supervised by the base officers, talked to the local villagers to see if they had any new information about Arabs in the area. The villagers told us that they had heard rumors that there were Arabs in the village where we were headed, but could offer no additional information.

After our talk with the villagers we walked down to the river to survey the crossing point. The water level was well above normal and the current was exceedingly swift. There was no way we could safely make a crossing there. The next crossing point wasn't for many miles, and we suspected it would also be impassable. Reluctantly the officer in charge decided to abort the mission, and we returned to the base.

Although the mission had been unsuccessful, I had enjoyed the outing down the picturesque Pech River Valley. It had been a mini-adventure for me, and I had seen some beautiful country. I wondered what would have happened if we had reached the village undetected where the suspected al-Qa'ida members were. We had a good tactical plan right out of the U.S. Army Ranger manual on how to approach undetected, and if necessary, assault the village to capture the al-Qa'ida members. How that plan would have worked out would forever remain a mystery.

The next day the base received a new mission objective. This time the target was a local Afghan timber dealer. The base wanted to talk to him because he was reported to be providing support to the Taliban. I joined the same contingent of base officers and Afghans on the drive to a narrow valley north of Asadabad where the timber dealer lived and owned a business. Upon arrival we dismounted the pickups and took up protected positions around the small compound while an Afghan and one of the base officers approached the front door and knocked. The timber dealer was not home, but the house servant didn't object when asked if we could come in and look around. Several of us went into the house and walked through each of its rooms looking for weapons or anything that might be of intelligence interest. The only thing we found was an old AK-47. As it was not unusual for Afghans to keep a gun in their homes, we did not confiscate it and left it where it was found.

On our return to base, my CIA colleagues wanted me to see the town of Asadabad, so we stopped in the central area of town and walked down a main street lined with shopping stalls and street vendors. At one food stall, which the base officers recommended, we stopped and purchased a local fried delicacy. By this point, a crowd of curious Afghans had begun to form around us. The Afghan team leader, concerned with our security, immediately began to shout and push the Afghans away. When one Afghan, an old man, did not move quickly enough, the team leader forcefully jabbed him in the chest with the end of the barrel of his AK-47, sending the man sprawling to the ground. I knew the blow had to hurt, and I felt badly that our presence had provoked the circumstances that led to the incident. The old Afghan got his retribution, however, although he never knew it. Within a few hours of eating the delicacy I would suffer the worst case of Montezuma's—or more appropriately, "Mohammad's"—revenge that I have ever experienced. It could have been worse, however. A few months after I returned to Headquarters I learned that the "bullet magnet" Afghan team leader had been shot and killed in an inter-tribal dispute.

* * *

My trip to Afghanistan had met my objectives. I felt I had a better understanding of the station's situation and the changed operational and inter-agency dynamics brought about by the much larger U.S. official presence there. The days of CIA teams partnered with small U.S. military elements roaming the countryside and operating in a near autonomous fashion were gone.

Back at Headquarters, unsurprisingly I found that not much had changed in my absence. On the political front, in the apparent interest of creating an effective central government in Afghanistan, many U.S. politicians and members of the media were continuing their calls to curtail U.S. support to Afghan militias and their leaders. These calls had begun almost immediately after the fall of the Taliban government. The Afghan leaders in question, often derisively referred to as "warlords" in the press, were the same ones on whom we had relied to act as surrogate ground forces to take on the Taliban and al-Qa'ida in 2001. In the wake of the overthrow of the Taliban government and in the absence of an effective Afghan Army, these leaders and their militias were stabilizing forces in Afghanistan, but this fact seemed to be lost on those calling for their immediate disbandment.

Also lost, or perhaps never acquired, was the understanding that real political and military power in Afghanistan resided at the local or regional level. Historically, this had always been true, and there was no reason to believe it would change just because the Taliban was no longer in charge and a U.S.–backed Afghan government was in power instead. Certainly, there was a role for the central government to play, as it had in Afghanistan's past, but the idea that we could quickly or easily impose a centralized, federal-style system of government on Afghanistan was a naïve and unsound one. Yet the drumbeat for disengagement from regional powerbrokers remained, and ultimately CIA did disengage completely or partially from many of the leaders with whom we had worked closely in 2001. The consequence was that with a declining ability for the CIA or other U.S. agencies to leverage and influence events at the regional level, a political and security vacuum began to develop. The Taliban has been seeking to refill that vacuum ever since.

*   *   *

My experience in and with Afghanistan has taught me that it is largely a primitive country, one whose culture does not mesh well with the modern world and democratic, liberal institutions. I believe a close analogy to the Afghanistan situation in relation to U.S. involvement can be found in America's history in the 1700's and 1800's when the country's westward continental expansion brought a modern industrialized nation up against what were essentially stone-age, tribal societies that had little conception of what lay beyond their homelands. This lack of understanding applied not only to geography but also to political concepts like nation-states, customs such as land ownership, or peace treaties written on paper. There was an equal lack of understanding of the Native American culture on the part of the U.S. government.

Given this great divide in culture, history, and industrial development, the U.S. government's interface with the Native American tribes was a disaster, with almost all of the consequences of that disaster occurring on the Native American side. The lack of knowledge and understanding of the American tribes certainly insured this result, with the effects carrying through to the present day. Similarly, our lack of an in-depth understanding of Afghan culture and history make it difficult for us to achieve the positive results we would like to see in seeking a stable Afghanistan for the long-term. Sadly, even when we as a government do understand the Afghan culture, we often seem incapable or unwilling to accept it for what it is, or factor that understanding into our policies and practices.

*   *   *

After 24 years of CIA service I retired in 2007 just two weeks after becoming eligible. I did so for a combination of reasons. One of those was because of the extraordinary experience I had in the fall of 2001 when I saw firsthand how people, a government, and a nation could come together and work unselfishly for the common good. In this regard, I knew that my experience with Foxtrot team and my journey to Kandahar, although born out of tragedy, would be the high point of my career, and it was something the likes of which I would never experience again. It was not going to get any better than that, nor be repeated in my professional career. It was time to move on.

Postscript 2017

In THE ENSUING 15 plus years since Kandahar fell, seemingly much has transpired in Afghanistan. Hamid Karzai, the soft-spoken Afghan I met that dark night at the airbase in Pakistan in November 2001, has taken his place in history, after serving for over 12 years as the leader of the country. During his tenure a new constitution was put in place, and a relatively large Western-trained, centrally-controlled military was established. Today, far more children are attending school than ever before, and the overall health of Afghanistan's people is significantly better as measured in life expectancy. From the U.S. national security perspective, the original, and in fact the only, objective at the outset of the U.S. intervention—ridding Afghanistan of al-Qa'ida—has been achieved, and was achieved quickly and early in what nonetheless has become America's longest war. These are no doubt positive developments of which the Afghans and the thousands of foreigners, military and civilian, who have helped to make them a reality, should be proud.

These accomplishments of course did not come without costs, both human and material, and it is not only fair but also right to ask, "Was it worth it?" The death of CIA officer Mike Spann in Mazar-e-Sharif in November 2001 was only the first American casualty in Afghanistan. His death was soon to be followed by the deaths of other courageous Americans as well as soldiers and civilians from allied nations. It began with a trickle of deaths perhaps, especially in those early years from 2001 to 2004, when around 158 Americans died. But even a trickle if it continues long enough can fill a bucket, and enough buckets can fill a barrel, and so it goes and has gone in Afghanistan. From 2005 to 2013, another approximately 2,857 Americans died. From 2014 to 2016, as the U.S. military drawdown first announced by

President Obama in 2011 began in earnest, casualties precipitously declined with another 116 Americans losing their lives. Small numbers perhaps, especially when compared to the conflicts in Vietnam and Korea, where in both cases the U.S. death toll reached scores of thousands. Even so, those numbers represent lost lives and much suffering for the affected families and friends.

The above numbers of course do not include the death toll of Afghans, which dwarfs the number of foreign soldiers. Nor does it include the number of wounded, many grievously, which is several times larger than the number of dead. Thus, despite these losses and the supreme sacrifices they represent, and despite the direct involvement of the militaries of the U.S. and other nations, and despite the sophistication and advanced military technology brought to bear, the old maxim "the graveyard of empires" continues to apply to Afghanistan. The land is still hard, the enemies found there are still tough, and military victory remains difficult and fleeting.

But the question remains: "Was it worth it?" Certainly the destruction of al-Qa'ida's sanctuary in Afghanistan, from which the worst attack in history against the U.S. homeland was planned and directed, was a required action. It had to be done. But as noted previously, this was accomplished very early on, certainly by the end of 2002, if not sooner, when the cost in American lives was only a fraction of the number it has reached in the years since. If the same question were asked at that point, when al-Qa'ida had been routed and was no longer active in Afghanistan, then it would be much easier to say, "Yes, it was worth it. A few courageous men died, but it was the price that had to be paid." But we did not stop after our goal was obtained. To give a satisfactory answer to the original question, we have to answer the additional questions of why did we stay and why so long? For it was in our lingering in Afghanistan that our greatest costs accrued.

After our initial success, and by ours I mean the U.S. and its allies, most notably the Afghans, there was clearly a need and opportunity to help get Afghanistan on its feet after many decades of war. I personally agreed with U.S. policy makers at the time that we could not simply walk away from Afghanistan as soon as our counterterrorism objective was accomplished. A stable and peaceful Afghanistan was seen as the best way to keep al-Qa'ida from regrouping in some remote corner of the country and emerging to again threaten the U.S. homeland. Afghanistan needed time to get its political house in order and to establish a functioning government, including a professional security service and military. The U.S. made the decision to help in this regard by committing additional combat troops and government advisors, and investing in the infrastructure of the country.

Although all of this went against President George W. Bush's declaration that Afghanistan would not become a nation-building exercise, the path the U.S. undertook was not an unreasonable one. It made sense as a strategy, and as we have noted, significant achievements can be cited with much of the credit due to the policy of continued U.S. involvement. It has not, however, resulted in peace. The Taliban is still in business, conducting conventional attacks and suicide operations with regularity, and perhaps most concerning, the presence of ISIS, the new al-Qa'ida, is on the rise.

So if the strategy of continued U.S. involvement in Afghanistan was sound, why after all these years has it not resulted in a peaceful and stable country? I believe there are many factors responsible for this. One of the primary ones was the U.S. invasion of Iraq, the results of which undermined our efforts in the critical early years in Afghanistan by shifting the U.S. focus, as well as resources, towards Iraq. This no doubt boosted the morale of the Taliban and other enemies in Afghanistan. More tangibly the shift caused a slow down of critical programs intended to help establish the new Afghan government and secure the country. In effect our efforts in Afghanistan went into a hold pattern. The result has been a much longer and protracted U.S. involvement in the country. The delays in implementing programs also allowed the Taliban to reconstitute itself as a potent insurgent force. Aiding and abetting in this new rise of the Taliban was the decision to stop supporting local militias, and the "warlords" that led them, before effective government security forces could be established, trained, and deployed. With the militias losing power, the Taliban was able to fill the vacuums that were created and reassert itself in many areas of the country. The U.S. responded ultimately to the rise of the Taliban by increasing combat forces by tens of thousands. But the damage had been done. Afghans lost confidence in the ability of their government to protect them, and the number of U.S. and allied dead and wounded rose dramatically.

But there were still other consequences for Afghanistan flowing from the U.S. decision to invade Iraq. ISIS, born out of the disintegration of the Middle East that stemmed from the U.S. overthrow of Saddam Hussein, is reported to have a presence in Afghanistan. An unintended consequence of our actions, no doubt, but a consequence nonetheless. The only positive thing that can be said about this development is that for now at least, ISIS and the Taliban appear to be competitors and not allies, unlike al-Qa'ida and the

Taliban. Let's hope this competition continues, as should their relationship improve, it could be the determining factor on how long the U.S. maintains a potent military force in Afghanistan.

So, has it been worth it? Sadly, I believe for the reasons laid out above, many of the lives lost and people wounded in Afghanistan could have been avoided if the U.S. had not invaded Iraq. In the interest of full disclosure, it was an invasion I did not support at the time. But does that mean the human sacrifice and treasure spent in Afghanistan has not been worth it? I think that depends on how and when the ongoing Taliban insurgency is resolved.

If nothing else, it should be clear at this point that the Taliban as a political and military force in Afghanistan is not going away. To defeat it militarily would require far more combat forces than the U.S. and its allies are likely willing to commit, especially after so many years of war. This being the case, a negotiated peace between the Taliban and the Afghan government that includes the participation of the U.S. is the only possible solution. America's primary goal in any such negotiation should be that no matter what form the resulting government takes, all parties to the settlement agree that no foreign extremist elements will be allowed to operate in Afghanistan. If they try to do so, the government, including any Taliban elements, will pursue them. Beyond this, all other issues and provisions should be up to the Afghan participants.

If, in the relative near future, an acceptable agreement is struck that ends the insurgency, brings peace and unity to Afghanistan, and guarantees that no extremists can gain sanctuary in the country and become a threat to the U.S. and its allies, then the answer to the question of "Has it been worth it?" is yes. Even as hard as those costs are to accept. If however, the Taliban insurgency continues with no end in sight, and particularly if ISIS is able to establish itself in Afghanistan and become a threat to the U.S., then no, it hasn't been worth it, and we will have squandered the huge sacrifices that were made on a lost cause.

Acknowledgments

I would never had been inspired to write this story were it not for the brave and determined service I witnessed in Pakistan and southern Afghanistan by the members of the CIA and Special Forces teams that participated in the campaign to capture Kandahar in 2001. The patriotism and professionalism of Foxtrot and Echo teams, and ODA-583 and ODA-574 were extraordinary, and I will forever cherish the memory of the events of that special time.

I also wish to recognize the critical support provided by the U.S. Air Force's 20th Special Operations Squadron and other U.S. military air support to the southern Afghanistan campaign without which success would have been doubtful. Additionally, I would be remiss not to acknowledge the men and women at CIA's Counterterrorist Center/Special Operations Group whose hard work in supporting our efforts from afar played an important role in making the campaign a success.

While the writing of a book is largely a solitary task, the help of others in making it better is indispensable. In this regard I owe my thanks to several people who read the manuscript and provided constructive criticism and encouragement. These include, Chuck Bertsch, Greg Gillam, Meg G., "Tomas," and Mike H. Additionally, I owe a special thanks to my wife who brought her considerable editorial talents to bear as well.

To my publisher, Theodore P. Savas, and Editorial Director Steven Smith, as well as the rest of the crew at Savas Beatie, I am deeply appreciative for the interest, time, and attention that have been given to the publication of my memoir.

Despite the help of others in producing this book, any errors or inaccuracies are my own.

Duane Evans is a former CIA officer with field tours on four continents including serving as Chief of Station, the CIA's most senior field position. He is the recipient of the Intelligence Star for valor and the Career Intelligence Medal. Prior to joining the Agency, Duane was a US Army Special Forces and Military Intelligence officer. A graduate of New Mexico State University, he is also the author of the acclaimed espionage novel *North From Calcutta*.